The Power of
COMPOUNDING

Achieving Exponential Wealth Growth through Investment Strategies ...

HENRY OTASOWERE

The Power of Compounding

©Copyright 2023 Henry Otasowere, "The Power of Compounding: Achieving Exponential Wealth Growth through Investment Strategies"

ALL RIGHTS RESERVED

No part of this publication may be reproduced, stored in a retrieval system, or transmitted, in any form or by any means, electronic, mechanical, photocopying, recording or otherwise, without the express written permission of the author.

Otimage Publishers

ISBN: 9798379117948

CONTENTS

Introduction 2
Why compounding is a powerful investment strategy 3
The benefits of long-term investing 6
Part 1 10
   Chapter 1 11
   The Basics of Compounding 11
      The Basics of Compounding: 11
      How compounding works 12
      Understanding the power of time in compounding 15
   Chapter 2 19
   The difference between simple interest and compound interest ... 19
      Expanding on the Topic: 19
Part 2 23
Investing in Stocks for Compounding 23
   Chapter 3 24
   Investing in Stocks for Compounding 24
      Introduction to stock investing 27
   Chapter 4 31
   How to select quality stocks for long-term investing 31
   Chapter 5 37
   Understanding dividends and dividend reinvestment plans 37
   Chapter 6 44
   Examples of successful long-term stock investors 44
Part 3 48
Bond Investing for Compounding 48
   Chapter 7 49
   Bond Investing for Compounding 49
      Introduction to bonds and bond investing 52
   Chapter 8 56

The different types of bonds and their risks 56
Strategies for using bonds in a compounding portfolio 59
How to reinvest bond income for maximum growth 61
Part 4 64
Cryptocurrency Investing for Compounding 64
Chapter 9 65
Cryptocurrency Investing for Compounding 65
Introduction to cryptocurrencies 68
Part 5 72
The potential for growth and risk in cryptocurrency investing 72
Chapter 10 73
The potential for growth and risk in cryptocurrency investing 73
Strategies for investing in cryptocurrencies for the long-term 76
Chapter 11 79
Examples of successful cryptocurrency investors 79
Part 6 82
Maximizing the Power of Compounding 82
Chapter 12 83
Maximizing the Power of Compounding 83
Developing a long-term investment plan 86
Here are a few things to keep in mind when developing a long-term investment plan: 88
How to manage risk in a compounding portfolio 89
Additional points to consider when managing risk in a compounding portfolio: 90
Chapter 13 92
The importance of patience and discipline in long-term investing . 92
Here are additional points on the importance of patience and discipline in long-term investing: 93
Use technology to your advantage 95
Some additional things people may not know about using technology to their advantage in investing: 96

- Don't try to time the market 97
- **Chapter 14** 100
- The importance of patience and discipline in long-term investing 100
  - Stick to your investment plan 101
  - Embrace volatility... 102
  - Diversify your portfolio 105
  - Be patient and don't get greedy 107
  - The potential pitfalls of short-term thinking and trading 108
- **Part 7** 110
- The power of compounding in achieving long-term wealth growth 110
- **Chapter 15** 111
- The power of compounding in achieving long-term wealth growth 111
  - Risk vs. reward 113
  - Why starting early and staying the course is key........................ 115
  - Final thoughts and recommendations 116

THE POWER OF
COMPOUNDING
"Achieving Exponential Wealth Growth through Investment Strategies"

Introduction

Investing is an essential part of building long-term wealth, and there are many strategies available to investors looking to grow their portfolios. One of the most powerful strategies is compounding, which allows investors to achieve exponential growth in their investments over time.

At its core, compounding is the idea of reinvesting your investment earnings, allowing them to generate more earnings over time. By reinvesting your earnings and taking advantage of the power of time, you can achieve significant growth in your investments, without having to take on excessive risk.

This book is designed to help you understand the power of compounding and how it can be used to achieve exponential wealth growth through various investment strategies. We'll explore the basics of compounding, the different types of investments that can be used in a compounding portfolio, and how to develop a long-term investment plan that takes advantage of the power of time.

Through real-world examples and practical guidance, you'll learn how to select quality stocks, bonds, and cryptocurrencies for long-term investment, how to reinvest your earnings for maximum growth, and how to manage risk in a compounding portfolio. Whether you're a new investor just starting out or a seasoned investor looking to optimize your long-term investment strategy, this book will provide valuable insights and guidance to help you achieve your investment goals.

Remember, compounding is a powerful tool, but it takes time and patience to realize its full potential. By starting early and staying disciplined, you can achieve exponential wealth growth and build a solid financial foundation for your future. Let's get started!

Why compounding is a powerful investment strategy

Compounding is a powerful investment strategy because it allows you to generate exponential growth in your investments over time. When you invest, you earn returns on your initial investment, as well as any returns that have been generated by your investment over time. By reinvesting those returns and allowing them to generate even more returns, you can achieve significant growth in your investments, without having to take on excessive risk.

The power of compounding is often referred to as the "eighth wonder of the world" and is attributed to Albert Einstein, who supposedly said that "compound interest is the most powerful force in the universe." While the quote may not be accurate, the sentiment is certainly true - compounding can have a profound impact on your investment returns over the long-term.

To illustrate the power of compounding, consider the following example: If you were to invest $10,000 in a stock that generates a 10% annual return, after one year, you would have $11,000. If you reinvested that $1,000 return and continued to earn a 10% return each year, after 10 years, you would have $25,937. By contrast, if you had simply taken the $1,000 return each year and spent it, you would have only $20,000 after 10 years. The difference in returns is significant, and it highlights the power of compounding over time.

The longer your investment time horizon, the more powerful compounding becomes. Even small differences in annual returns can have a significant impact on your investment returns over the long-term. By reinvesting your returns and staying disciplined over the long-term, you can achieve exponential growth in your investments and build a solid financial foundation for your future.

In addition to the potential for exponential growth, compounding has other advantages as well. One of the key benefits is that it allows investors to take a long-term approach to investing. By reinvesting earnings and staying invested over the long-term, investors can ride out market volatility and benefit from the power of time. This is particularly important in the stock market, where short-term fluctuations can be significant, but long-term trends tend to be more predictable.

Another benefit of compounding is that it can help investors to achieve their financial goals more efficiently. Because compounding generates returns on returns, it allows investors to achieve higher returns on their investments with less money invested upfront. This can be particularly beneficial for investors who are just starting out and may not have a significant amount of capital to invest.

Compounding can also be an effective tool for managing risk in an investment portfolio. By reinvesting earnings, investors can diversify their portfolio and reduce their exposure to individual stocks or sectors. This can help to minimize the impact of market volatility and protect investors from significant losses.

Overall, the power of compounding is an essential concept for investors to understand. By reinvesting earnings and staying invested over the long-term, investors can achieve exponential growth in their investments, take a more long-term approach to investing, achieve their financial goals more efficiently, and manage risk in their portfolio. Whether you're a new investor just starting out or a seasoned investor looking to optimize your investment strategy, understanding the power of compounding is critical to building a successful investment portfolio.

It's also worth noting that compounding is not just limited to one type of investment. It can be applied to a variety of investment vehicles, including stocks, bonds, mutual funds, ETFs, and even cryptocurrencies. This means that investors have a wide range of options when it comes to building a compounding investment portfolio, allowing them to tailor their investments to their unique goals, risk tolerance, and investment timeline.

Another important factor to consider when using compounding as an investment strategy is the impact of fees and taxes. Fees can eat into investment returns, and taxes can reduce the power of compounding over time. To maximize the benefits of compounding, investors should look for investment vehicles with low fees and be strategic in their tax planning. For example, investing in tax-advantaged accounts like 401(k)s, IRAs, and Roth IRAs can help to minimize the impact of taxes on investment returns.

Compounding is a powerful investment strategy that can help investors achieve exponential growth in their investments over time. It's a long-term approach to investing that allows investors to ride out market volatility, achieve their financial goals more efficiently, and manage risk in their portfolio. By understanding the power of compounding and being strategic in their investment decisions, investors can build a strong investment portfolio that can help them achieve financial security and success over the long-term.

The benefits of long-term investing

The benefits of long-term investing are often overlooked or underestimated, and many people do not fully understand the advantages that a long-term approach can offer. One of the most significant benefits of long-term investing is the power of compounding, as we have previously discussed. By allowing your investments to compound over time, you can achieve exponential growth in your portfolio, and potentially generate significant returns that would not be possible with a short-term approach.

However, compounding is just one of the many benefits of long-term investing. Another key advantage is the ability to ride out short-term market volatility and benefit from long-term trends. In the short-term, the stock market can be unpredictable, and prices can fluctuate significantly based on a wide range of factors, such as economic conditions, political events, and global developments. But over the long-term, the market tends to follow certain trends and can be more predictable. By taking a long-term approach, investors can benefit from these long-term trends, even if they experience short-term fluctuations along the way.

Another benefit of long-term investing is the ability to diversify your portfolio and reduce risk. By investing in a wide range of assets and sectors, you can reduce the impact of individual stocks or sectors on your overall portfolio. This can help to minimize the impact of market volatility and protect you from significant losses. Additionally, diversification can help to generate more consistent returns over the long-term, as different assets will perform differently at different times.

Another advantage of long-term investing is the ability to reduce costs and maximize returns. By taking a buy-and-hold approach, you can avoid the costs associated with frequent trading, such as commissions, fees, and taxes. These costs can add up over time and can significantly impact your overall returns. Additionally, long-term investing allows you to take advantage of the power of dollar-cost averaging, where you invest a fixed amount of money at regular intervals. This can help you to buy more shares when prices are low and fewer shares when prices are high, ultimately maximizing your overall returns.

The benefits of long-term investing are numerous and significant. By taking a long-term approach to investing, you can benefit from the power of compounding, ride out short-term market volatility, diversify your portfolio, reduce costs, and maximize returns. While short-term investing can offer the potential for quick profits, the risks are also higher, and the potential for sustainable growth is limited. Long-term investing is a more sustainable and secure approach that can help you achieve your financial goals and build long-term wealth.

It's important to note that long-term investing requires patience and discipline. It's not a get-rich-quick scheme, and it may take many years before you see significant returns on your investments. But by taking a long-term approach and sticking to a well-diversified investment plan, you can build a strong portfolio that can weather short-term market fluctuations and generate consistent returns over time.

Another thing that many people don't realize is that the emotional aspect of investing can play a significant role in long-term success. The stock market can be unpredictable and volatile, and it's easy to become emotional and make impulsive investment decisions based on short-term market movements. But by taking a long-term approach and focusing on the fundamentals of the companies and assets in your portfolio, you can avoid the emotional rollercoaster of the stock market and make informed, rational investment decisions that will benefit you in the long run.

It's worth noting that long-term investing isn't just for wealthy individuals or those with a lot of experience in the stock market. Anyone can take a long-term approach to investing, regardless of their income level or investment experience. In fact, starting early and taking a long-term approach can be especially beneficial for young investors, as they have more time to benefit from the power of compounding.

The benefits of long-term investing are numerous and significant, but they require patience, discipline, and a focus on the fundamentals. By taking a long-term approach to investing, you can benefit from the power of compounding, ride out short-term market volatility, diversify your portfolio, reduce costs, and maximize returns. And while the emotional aspects of investing can be challenging, sticking to a well-diversified investment plan can help you achieve your financial goals and build long-term wealth.

PART 1
The Basics of Compounding

CHAPTER *1*

THE BASICS OF COMPOUNDING

If you're interested in building long-term wealth, then understanding the basics of compounding is crucial. Compounding is a simple but powerful investment strategy that can help you achieve exponential growth in your investments over time. By reinvesting your earnings, you allow them to compound, which means that your investments generate earnings that are then reinvested to generate even more earnings. This creates a snowball effect that can lead to significant growth in your investments over the long-term.

In this chapter, we'll take a closer look at the basics of compounding, including what it is, how it works, and why it's such a powerful investment strategy. We'll also provide some examples to help illustrate the concept and show you how you can start applying it to your own investment portfolio.

The Basics of Compounding:

Compounding is a simple concept, but it can be a bit difficult to grasp at first. Essentially, it's the process of reinvesting your earnings to generate even more earnings. Here's how it works:

Let's say you invest $10,000 in a stock that pays a 5% annual dividend. After the first year, you would receive $500 in dividends. If you reinvest that $500 back into the same stock, you now have a total investment of $10,500. The following year, the stock pays another 5% dividend, but this time, it's based on the higher investment amount. So now, you would receive $525 in dividends. If you reinvest that $525 back into the same stock, your investment would now be worth $11,025. This process repeats itself year after year, and as your investment grows, so do your earnings.

The key to compounding is that it generates exponential growth. In the example above, your investment grew by $25 in the second year, which may not seem like a lot. But over time, which growth compounds on itself, leading to significant returns. In fact, over a 30-year period, that initial investment of $10,000 could grow to over $43,000, assuming a 5% annual return.

One of the reasons compounding is such a powerful investment strategy is that it allows you to generate returns on your earnings, not just on your initial investment. This can lead to significant growth in your portfolio over time. And the longer you allow your investments to compound, the greater the potential for growth.

Compounding is a powerful investment strategy that can help you achieve significant growth in your portfolio over the long-term. By reinvesting your earnings and allowing them to compound, you can generate exponential returns that would not be possible with a short-term approach. While it can be challenging to grasp at first, the basics of compounding are simple, and anyone can start applying this strategy to their own investment portfolio. By understanding the power of compounding, you can take the first step towards building long-term wealth and achieving your financial goals.

How compounding works

Compounding is a simple but powerful investment strategy that can help you achieve exponential growth in your investments over time. It works by reinvesting the earnings or returns generated from an investment, and then earning returns on both the initial investment and the reinvested earnings. This process repeats itself, generating a snowball effect that can lead to significant growth in your investments over time.

What many people may not know is that compounding is most effective when it is allowed to work over a long period of time. The longer the time horizon, the greater the potential for growth. This is because compounding generates exponential returns, meaning that the returns generated in one period become the base for the next period's returns, and so on.

For example, let's say you invest $10,000 in a stock that generates a 10% annual return. After one year, your investment is worth $11,000. If you reinvest the $1,000 return back into the same stock, your investment will be worth $12,100 after the second year. After the third year, your investment will be worth $13,310, and so on. As you can see, the returns generated in each subsequent year are not just on the original $10,000 investment but also on the returns generated in previous years.

Another important aspect of compounding is the power of compounding frequency. This refers to how often the returns are reinvested. The more frequent the compounding, the greater the potential for growth. For example, if the returns are reinvested quarterly instead of annually, the growth rate will be higher because the reinvested returns will start earning returns sooner.

It's also worth noting that compounding can work in reverse, which can have a significant impact on your investments. If you have debt that charges interest, the interest charges can compound over time, making it harder to pay off the debt. This is why it's important to not only focus on growing your investments but also on managing your debt.

In conclusion, compounding is a powerful investment strategy that can help you achieve significant growth in your investments over time. By reinvesting your earnings and allowing them to compound, you can generate exponential returns that would not be possible with a short-term approach. The key is to allow compounding to work over a long period of time and to be mindful of the impact of compounding in both positive and negative contexts.

Another thing that many people may not know about compounding is the importance of starting early. The earlier you start, the more time you have to allow compounding to work its magic. This is because the longer your money has to grow, the greater the potential for compounding returns. Starting early also means that you can start with smaller investments and still achieve significant growth over time.

It's also important to understand the role of risk and return in compounding. In general, investments that have higher returns also tend to be riskier. While the potential for higher returns may be appealing, it's important to consider the risks involved and make sure that you are comfortable with the level of risk in your investments. A higher risk investment may experience greater volatility, which can lead to larger fluctuations in the value of your investment, and this can impact the compounding effect.

Furthermore, it's important to keep in mind that compounding is not a guarantee of investment success. Even though the potential for significant growth is there, there is no guarantee that an investment will perform well over time. It's important to diversify your investments and to have a well-rounded investment strategy that takes into account your risk tolerance, financial goals, and time horizon.

Understanding how compounding works is essential for any investor looking to achieve long-term wealth growth. The benefits of compounding are significant, but it's important to have a long-term perspective, to start early, to consider the impact of compounding frequency, to balance risk and return, and to have a well-diversified investment strategy. With these key principles in mind, you can harness the power of compounding and make the most of your investments over time.

Understanding the power of time in compounding

Time is an essential element in the power of compounding. As we have discussed, compounding works by reinvesting the earnings or returns generated from an investment, which then generates additional returns over time. The longer you allow this process to continue, the greater the potential for exponential growth.

What many people don't realize is just how much of an impact time can have on the compounding effect. Even small differences in the length of time that an investment is allowed to compound can have a significant impact on the final value of the investment.

For example, let's say you invest $10,000 in a stock that generates a 10% annual return. If you allow the investment to compound for 10 years, it will be worth $25,937. However, if you allow the investment to compound for 20 years, it will be worth $67,275. This is due to the power of exponential growth, which accelerates the growth rate of the investment over time.

Another important factor to consider is the impact of inflation on the compounding effect. Inflation erodes the purchasing power of money over time, which can impact the value of the returns generated by an investment. However, over long periods of time, the compounding effect can help to offset the impact of inflation and generate real growth in the value of the investment.

It's also worth noting that the power of time in compounding is closely linked to the concept of "time value of money." This concept recognizes that money today is worth more than money in the future because it can be invested and earn returns. Therefore, the longer you allow your money to compound, the greater the potential for it to increase in value.

Understanding the power of time in compounding is essential for any investor looking to achieve long-term wealth growth. The longer you allow your investments to compound, the greater the potential for exponential growth. By starting early, investing consistently, and allowing time to work its magic, you can harness the power of compounding and achieve your financial goals over the long term. However, it's important to keep in mind the impact of inflation and to have a well-diversified investment strategy that takes into account your risk tolerance, financial goals, and time horizon.

Another important aspect to consider when it comes to the power of time in compounding is the impact of compounding frequency. In most cases, the more frequently an investment compounds, the greater the potential for exponential growth.

For example, let's say you invest $10,000 in a stock that generates a 10% annual return. If the investment compounds annually, after 10 years, it will be worth $25,937. However, if the investment compounds quarterly, after 10 years, it will be worth $27,086. This is because the more frequently the investment compounds, the more opportunities there are for the returns to generate additional returns.

Another thing that many people may not know is the importance of avoiding unnecessary fees and expenses. Fees and expenses can eat away at the returns generated by an investment and reduce the impact of compounding. For example, if an investment generates a 10% return but has a 2% expense ratio, the effective return will only be 8%. Over time, this can have a significant impact on the final value of the investment.

It's also worth noting that the power of time in compounding is not limited to any one particular type of investment. Compounding can be applied to a wide range of investment vehicles, including stocks, bonds, mutual funds, and other types of assets. The key is to choose investments that are aligned with your financial goals, risk tolerance, and time horizon, and to allow them to compound over the long term.

Understanding the power of time in compounding is essential for any investor looking to achieve long-term wealth growth. By allowing your investments to compound over a long period of time, you can harness the power of exponential growth and achieve your financial goals. However, it's important to keep in mind the impact of compounding frequency, fees and expenses, and to have a well-diversified investment strategy that takes into account your risk tolerance, financial goals, and time horizon.

Another important aspect of understanding the power of time in compounding is the concept of opportunity cost. This refers to the cost of not investing your money, and the potential returns you could have earned if you had invested it instead.

For example, let's say you have $10,000 in cash that you're considering investing. If you choose to leave that money in a savings account that earns a 1% annual return, after 10 years, your investment will be worth $11,046. However, if you invest that money in a stock that generates a 10% annual return, after 10 years, your investment will be worth $25,937.

In this scenario, the opportunity cost of leaving your money in a savings account is significant, as you could have earned much higher returns by investing in a more growth-oriented asset. This is why it's important to consider the potential opportunity cost of not investing when making financial decisions.

It's also important to note that the power of time in compounding is not limited to only investing large sums of money. Even small amounts of money invested consistently over a long period of time can lead to significant wealth growth. For example, investing $100 per month in a stock that generates a 10% annual return over a period of 30 years would result in a final investment value of over $190,000.

Understanding the power of time in compounding is key to achieving long-term wealth growth through investing. By investing early and consistently, and allowing your investments to compound over time, you can harness the power of exponential growth and achieve your financial goals. However, it's important to consider the opportunity cost of not investing and to have a well-diversified investment strategy that takes into account your risk tolerance, financial goals, and time horizon.

CHAPTER *2*

THE DIFFERENCE BETWEEN SIMPLE INTEREST AND COMPOUND INTEREST

When it comes to understanding how money grows, it's important to understand the difference between simple interest and compound interest. Simple interest is calculated on the principal amount of an investment or loan, while compound interest is calculated on the principal amount as well as the accumulated interest. Understanding the difference between these two types of interest is crucial for making informed investment decisions and maximizing your wealth over time.

Expanding on the Topic:

Many people may not know that the difference between simple interest and compound interest can have a significant impact on the growth of their investments. With simple interest, the interest earned on an investment is based solely on the principal amount, and does not take into account any interest earned in previous periods. This means that the growth of the investment is linear and does not accelerate over time.

On the other hand, with compound interest, the interest earned on an investment is added to the principal amount, and interest is then earned on the new, higher total. This means that the growth of the investment is exponential, and over time, the interest earned on the investment can become a significant portion of the total value.

For example, let's say you invest $10,000 in a savings account that earns a 5% annual simple interest rate. After one year, your investment will be worth $10,500. However, if you invest the same amount in an account that earns a 5% annual compound interest rate, after one year, your investment will be worth $10,525.25. Over time, the difference in growth between simple interest and compound interest can become significant, and can impact the final value of an investment.

It's also important to note that the difference between simple interest and compound interest is not limited to only savings accounts or low-risk investments. It can also apply to other types of investments, including stocks, bonds, and other securities. Understanding the type of interest calculation used for a particular investment is crucial for making informed decisions and maximizing wealth growth over time.

The difference between simple interest and compound interest is a fundamental concept in finance that is essential for understanding how investments grow over time. By understanding the power of compound interest and how it differs from simple interest, investors can make informed decisions and maximize their wealth growth potential.

Many people may also not know that the power of compound interest is amplified by the length of time that an investment is held. The longer an investment is allowed to compound, the greater the impact on its growth. This is why starting early and allowing investments to compound over a long period of time can be so beneficial for investors.

For example, let's say you invest $10,000 in a savings account that earns a 5% annual compound interest rate. If you leave the investment alone for 10 years, it will be worth $16,386.17.

However, if you leave the investment alone for 30 years, it will be worth $43,219.96. This demonstrates the power of time in compounding and the significant impact that it can have on investment growth.

Another aspect of compound interest that many people may not be aware of is the concept of compounding frequency. This refers to how often the interest on an investment is compounded. The more frequently the interest is compounded, the faster the investment will grow. For example, an investment that compounds interest monthly will grow faster than an investment that compounds interest annually, all other factors being equal.

Understanding the difference between simple interest and compound interest is just the first step in understanding the power of compounding. It is important to also consider the impact of time and compounding frequency on investment growth. By understanding these concepts, investors can make informed decisions and maximize their wealth growth potential over the long term.

It's also worth noting that compound interest is not just limited to savings accounts or bank deposits. It can also be applied to other types of investments such as stocks, bonds, and mutual funds. In fact, compound interest is a key factor in the growth of the stock market over the long term.

One important thing to keep in mind when investing is the impact of fees on the compounding effect. Investment fees, such as management fees, commissions, and trading fees, can eat into the growth of an investment over time. It's important to carefully consider the fees associated with any investment and to look for low-cost options that allow for maximum growth potential.

Finally, it's important to note that while compound interest can be a powerful tool for wealth growth, it is not a guarantee of returns. Investments are subject to market fluctuations and there is always a risk of loss. It's important to have a diversified portfolio and to carefully consider risk tolerance and investment goals when making investment decisions.

Understanding the difference between simple and compound interest is just the beginning. The true power of compounding lies in its ability to exponentially grow wealth over time, but it's important to consider factors such as time, compounding frequency, fees, and risk when making investment decisions. By doing so, investors can take advantage of the power of compounding and achieve long-term financial success.

PART 2

Investing in Stocks for Compounding

Chapter 3
INVESTING IN STOCKS FOR COMPOUNDING

Investing in stocks for compounding is a popular investment strategy that has the potential to generate significant returns over the long term. The strategy involves investing in stocks and allowing the earnings to compound over time, generating exponential growth in wealth. However, there are many aspects of this strategy that many people may not know about.

One of the key benefits of investing in stocks for compounding is the potential for high returns. Historically, the stock market has generated higher returns than other investment options such as bonds or savings accounts. Additionally, investing in individual stocks allows investors to capitalize on the growth potential of specific companies.

Another important aspect of investing in stocks for compounding is the need for a long-term investment horizon. The stock market is inherently volatile, with prices fluctuating on a daily basis. However, over the long term, the market has consistently trended upwards, generating significant returns for patient investors. This means that investors should be prepared to hold their investments for many years, if not decades, to fully capitalize on the compounding effect.

Many people may also not know that diversification is crucial when investing in stocks for compounding. By investing in a diversified portfolio of stocks across different industries, investors can reduce their risk exposure while still capturing the growth potential of the market. Additionally, it's important to regularly review and rebalance a stock portfolio to ensure that it remains diversified and aligned with investment goals.

Another important consideration when investing in stocks for compounding is the impact of fees and taxes on investment growth. Trading fees, management fees, and taxes can all eat into the returns generated by a stock portfolio over time. It's important to carefully consider these factors and to look for low-cost investment options, such as index funds, that can provide exposure to the stock market with minimal fees.

Investing in stocks for compounding can be a powerful strategy for generating long-term wealth growth. However, it's important to understand the risks and benefits of this strategy and to carefully consider factors such as diversification, fees, taxes, and investment horizon. By doing so, investors can take advantage of the growth potential of the stock market while minimizing their risk exposure and maximizing their potential for long-term financial success.

Another key aspect of investing in stocks for compounding is the importance of conducting thorough research and analysis before making investment decisions. This involves looking into the financial health and performance of individual companies and assessing their growth potential, competitive position, and management team. Additionally, investors should keep up-to-date on market trends, economic indicators, and geopolitical events that can impact the performance of the stock market and individual companies.

One aspect that many people may not know about when investing in stocks for compounding is the impact of dividend reinvestment on long-term returns. Many companies pay out regular dividends to their shareholders, which can be reinvested back into the company through a dividend reinvestment plan. This allows investors to take advantage of the compounding effect of their dividend earnings, generating even higher returns over the long term.

Investors should also be aware of the impact of market cycles and economic downturns on their stock investments. While the stock market has historically generated strong returns over the long term, it is also subject to market cycles and occasional downturns. Investors should be prepared to weather these fluctuations and hold their investments for the long term to maximize the potential for compounding returns.

Investors should also consider the impact of behavioral biases on their investment decisions. Emotional decision-making, such as reacting to short-term market fluctuations or following the herd mentality, can lead to poor investment outcomes and undermine the potential for long-term growth through compounding.

Investing in stocks for compounding is a powerful strategy for generating long-term wealth growth. However, it requires a thorough understanding of the risks and benefits of the strategy, as well as a commitment to ongoing research, analysis, and disciplined decision-making. By taking these factors into account, investors can maximize their potential for compounding returns and achieve long-term financial success.

Another aspect that many people may not know about when investing in stocks for compounding is the importance of diversification. Investing in a single stock or industry can be risky, as a decline in the performance of that particular stock or industry can have a significant impact on the value of the investment portfolio. Diversification involves spreading investments across different stocks, industries, and asset classes to reduce risk and increase the potential for long-term growth.

Investors should also consider the impact of fees and expenses on their investment returns. While fees and expenses may seem small, they can add up over time and significantly reduce the potential for compounding returns. It is important for investors to be aware of the fees associated with their investment accounts, such as management fees, transaction fees, and account maintenance fees, and to seek out low-cost investment options wherever possible.

Investors should also be aware of the impact of taxes on their investment returns. In particular, capital gains taxes can significantly impact the value of an investment portfolio over time. By strategically managing their investments, such as holding onto stocks for longer periods of time to qualify for long-term capital gains tax rates, investors can minimize the impact of taxes on their investment returns and maximize the potential for compounding growth.

Investors should also consider the impact of their personal financial goals and risk tolerance on their investment decisions. While compounding returns can generate significant wealth over the long term, it is important for investors to ensure that their investment strategy aligns with their financial goals and risk tolerance. This may involve working with a financial advisor to develop a personalized investment plan that takes into account factors such as age, income, expenses, and time horizon.

Overall, investing in stocks for compounding can be a powerful strategy for generating long-term wealth growth. However, it requires a thorough understanding of the risks and benefits of the strategy, as well as a commitment to ongoing research, analysis, and disciplined decision-making. By taking these factors into account, investors can maximize their potential for compounding returns and achieve long-term financial success.

Introduction to stock investing

Stock investing is a powerful strategy for building wealth over the long term. By investing in stocks, individuals have the opportunity to own a portion of a company and benefit from its growth and profitability over time. However, the world of stock investing can be complex and intimidating, especially for those who are new to the practice. In this section, we will provide an introduction to stock investing, as well as insights into what many people do not know about this topic.

One of the things that many people do not realize about stock investing is that it can be accessible to investors of all levels of experience and income. While some may believe that investing in the stock market is only for the wealthy or for professional investors, the reality is that there are many low-cost investment options available for individuals who are just starting out. For example, many online brokerages offer low-cost trading fees, and some even offer commission-free trading for certain types of investments.

Another misconception about stock investing is that it is inherently risky. While there is certainly risk involved in any investment, including stocks, there are also many strategies that investors can use to manage and minimize risk. For example, investors can diversify their portfolios by investing in a range of different stocks and asset classes, which can help to reduce the impact of a decline in the performance of any one particular investment.

Many people also underestimate the impact of taxes on their investment returns. In particular, capital gains taxes can significantly impact the value of an investment portfolio over time. By strategically managing their investments, such as holding onto stocks for longer periods of time to qualify for long-term capital gains tax rates, investors can minimize the impact of taxes on their investment returns and maximize the potential for long-term growth.

It is important for investors to keep in mind that stock investing is a long-term strategy. While there may be short-term fluctuations in the performance of individual stocks or the market as a whole, over the long term, stocks have historically provided strong returns. By staying disciplined and committed to their investment strategy over time, investors can benefit from the power of compounding and achieve their financial goals.

Stock investing can be a powerful tool for building long-term wealth. By understanding the accessibility of stock investing, managing risk, minimizing taxes, and maintaining a long-term perspective, investors can benefit from the potential growth and profitability that stocks can offer.

Another important aspect to consider in stock investing is the importance of doing thorough research before investing in any company. While it can be tempting to jump into a stock based on a hot tip or a recommendation from a friend, it is critical to do your own due diligence and research the company thoroughly before investing. This can include looking at the company's financial statements, understanding its business model and competitive advantages, and analyzing the broader market and industry trends that could impact the company's performance.

In addition, many people do not realize that there are different types of stocks that can offer different levels of risk and potential return. For example, growth stocks are often associated with high-growth companies that may not yet be profitable but have the potential for significant future growth. Value stocks, on the other hand, are often associated with established, profitable companies that may be trading at a discount relative to their earnings or assets. By understanding the different types of stocks and the associated risks and potential rewards, investors can tailor their investment strategies to their individual goals and risk tolerance.

Another common misconception about stock investing is that it is a zero-sum game, meaning that for one investor to win, another investor must lose. While there may be winners and losers on individual trades, the stock market as a whole has historically provided strong returns over the long term, benefiting all investors who participate. By focusing on long-term growth and staying disciplined in their investment strategy, investors can benefit from the overall growth of the market and achieve their financial goals.

It is important to consider the impact of fees and expenses on investment returns. While some investment fees, such as trading fees or management fees, may be necessary to access certain investments or services, others, such as high expense ratios on mutual funds, can significantly eat into investment returns over time. By being aware of the fees and expenses associated with their investments and seeking out low-cost options where possible, investors can maximize their potential returns and achieve their financial goals more efficiently.

There are many misconceptions and misunderstandings about stock investing. By understanding the accessibility of stock investing, doing thorough research, tailoring investment strategies to individual goals and risk tolerance, staying disciplined, and minimizing fees and expenses, investors can harness the power of compounding and achieve their financial goals through stock investing.

CHAPTER *4*

HOW TO SELECT QUALITY STOCKS FOR LONG-TERM INVESTING

When it comes to selecting quality stocks for long-term investing, there are many factors to consider beyond just the company's financial performance. While analyzing financial statements and profitability ratios can provide a good starting point, there are other important considerations that many people may not be aware of.

One important factor to consider when selecting quality stocks is the company's competitive advantages, also known as moats. A company with a strong moat has a sustainable competitive advantage that allows it to outperform its peers over the long term. This can include factors such as proprietary technology, economies of scale, or a strong brand reputation. By identifying companies with strong moats, investors can select stocks with a higher likelihood of long-term success.

Another important consideration is the company's management team. A skilled and experienced management team can help ensure that the company is well-positioned for long-term success and can weather market downturns and other challenges. When researching potential stocks, investors should look at the company's leadership team, their track record, and their strategic vision for the company.

In addition, many people may not be aware of the importance of considering broader industry and market trends when selecting quality stocks for long-term investing. While individual company performance is important, it is also crucial to consider how the company fits within its broader market and industry. By analyzing market trends, understanding industry dynamics, and identifying emerging technologies or disruptors, investors can select stocks that are well-positioned for long-term growth and success.

It is important to consider valuation when selecting quality stocks for long-term investing. While a company with a strong moat and strong financial performance may seem like a great investment, it may not be a good investment if the stock is overvalued. By analyzing a company's price-to-earnings ratio, price-to-sales ratio, and other valuation metrics, investors can ensure that they are paying a fair price for the company's potential future earnings.

When selecting quality stocks for long-term investing, it is important to consider factors beyond just financial performance. By analyzing a company's competitive advantages, management team, industry and market trends, and valuation, investors can select stocks that are well-positioned for long-term growth and success. By staying disciplined and focusing on long-term goals, investors can harness the power of compounding and achieve their financial objectives through stock investing.

Another important consideration that many people may overlook when selecting quality stocks for long-term investing is the company's sustainability and social responsibility. With a growing focus on environmental, social, and governance (ESG) factors, investors are increasingly looking for companies that prioritize sustainability and corporate responsibility.

By investing in companies with strong ESG practices, investors can not only support more responsible business practices but also potentially benefit from stronger long-term financial performance. Companies with strong sustainability practices may be better positioned to manage risks and opportunities related to environmental and social issues, attract and retain top talent, and build brand reputation and consumer loyalty.

Investors can also benefit from considering macroeconomic factors when selecting quality stocks for long-term investing. While it is important to focus on individual company performance and fundamentals, it is also important to understand how broader economic trends and policies may impact the company's future prospects. For example, changes in interest rates, inflation, or government regulations can all have significant impacts on a company's financial performance and stock price.

It is important for investors to have a long-term perspective when selecting quality stocks. While short-term market fluctuations and news headlines may be unsettling, a focus on long-term goals and fundamentals can help investors stay disciplined and avoid making rash decisions based on emotion or market noise. By investing in quality companies with strong fundamentals and competitive advantages, and maintaining a long-term focus, investors can harness the power of compounding and potentially achieve significant wealth growth over time.

Another important factor to consider when selecting quality stocks for long-term investing is the company's management team. A strong and experienced management team can be crucial in ensuring a company's long-term success and sustainability. Look for companies with a proven track record of delivering consistent earnings growth, increasing dividends, and making smart investments for future growth.

It is also important to consider a company's competitive position and industry dynamics. Companies operating in industries with high barriers to entry and strong competitive advantages, such as brand recognition or patents, may be better positioned to maintain their market position and profitability over the long term.

Another thing that many people may not realize is the importance of diversification when investing in individual stocks. While investing in a few high-quality companies may seem like a sound strategy, it also exposes investors to significant concentration risk if one of those companies underperforms or faces unforeseen challenges. Diversifying across multiple stocks and industries can help spread risk and potentially reduce the impact of any individual company's underperformance.

Investors should also be mindful of valuation when selecting quality stocks for long-term investing. While it is important to focus on the company's long-term potential, overpaying for a stock can limit the potential for future gains and increase the risk of loss. Using fundamental analysis and metrics such as price-to-earnings ratios, price-to-book ratios, and dividend yields can help investors evaluate whether a stock is priced appropriately relative to its earnings and growth potential.

Selecting quality stocks for long-term investing requires careful consideration of a range of factors, from company fundamentals and sustainability practices to industry dynamics and valuation. By investing in high-quality companies with strong management teams, competitive advantages, and long-term growth potential, and maintaining a diversified portfolio with a long-term focus, investors can harness the power of compounding and potentially achieve significant wealth growth over time.

It's important for investors to also consider the macroeconomic environment and how it may impact their chosen stocks. For example, changes in interest rates, inflation, and global economic conditions can all have an impact on company earnings and stock prices. It's important to stay informed and be able to adapt your investment strategy as market conditions change.

Additionally, many people may not realize the benefits of investing in exchange-traded funds (ETFs) or mutual funds, which offer a more diversified approach to stock investing. These funds hold a portfolio of stocks and provide exposure to a range of companies and industries, which can help mitigate the risk of individual stock underperformance. ETFs and mutual funds also offer the potential for compounding and long-term growth, while providing more convenient and cost-effective access to the stock market for many individual investors.

Investors should also be aware of the potential pitfalls of stock investing, including market volatility, corporate scandals, and unexpected changes in government regulations or consumer trends. It's important to have a clear investment strategy and risk management plan in place, and to avoid making emotional investment decisions based on short-term market fluctuations.

While stock investing can offer the potential for compounding and significant long-term wealth growth, it requires careful consideration of a range of factors and a disciplined, long-term approach. By focusing on quality companies with strong fundamentals, diversifying across multiple stocks and industries, and staying informed about market conditions and macroeconomic factors, investors can make sound investment decisions and potentially achieve their long-term financial goals.

One more thing to consider when selecting quality stocks for long-term investing is the company's management team. A strong, experienced management team that has a clear vision for the company's future can help ensure its long-term success and growth potential. Look for companies that have a history of delivering consistent earnings and revenue growth, and that have a track record of effectively managing their finances and resources.

Another factor to consider is a company's competitive advantage, or "moat". A company with a strong competitive advantage is able to fend off competitors and maintain its market share over the long term. Look for companies that have a unique product or service offering, strong brand recognition, and a sustainable business model.

It's also important to consider a company's valuation and growth potential. Look for companies that are trading at a reasonable price relative to their earnings and cash flow, and that have the potential for future growth. This may involve researching industry trends, analyzing financial statements, and monitoring analyst reports and news updates.

Investors should be prepared to hold onto their stocks for the long term and weather short-term market volatility. Investing in quality stocks for the purpose of compounding requires a long-term mindset and a willingness to ride out market fluctuations. With patience and discipline, investors can potentially achieve significant long-term wealth growth through stock investing and the power of compounding.

CHAPTER 5

UNDERSTANDING DIVIDENDS AND DIVIDEND REINVESTMENT PLANS

When investing in stocks, one way to potentially enhance the power of compounding is by investing in companies that pay dividends. A dividend is a distribution of a portion of a company's earnings to its shareholders. Many companies pay dividends on a regular basis, typically quarterly or annually.

One important thing to understand about dividends is that they can potentially provide a stable source of income for investors, regardless of market conditions. Additionally, companies that pay consistent dividends may be more stable and financially sound, which can be attractive to long-term investors.

Another important aspect of dividend investing is dividend reinvestment plans (DRIPs). A DRIP is a program offered by many companies that allows investors to automatically reinvest their dividends into additional shares of the company's stock, rather than receiving the dividends as cash. This can potentially enhance the power of compounding by allowing investors to continually reinvest their earnings and benefit from the growth potential of the company.

Many investors are not aware of the benefits of DRIPs and may not take advantage of this opportunity to maximize their returns. Additionally, some investors may not fully understand how to enroll in a DRIP or the potential tax implications of reinvesting dividends, so it's important to do research and seek guidance from a financial advisor before making any investment decisions.

Understanding dividends and DRIPs can be a powerful tool for investors looking to maximize the power of compounding. By investing in quality companies that pay consistent dividends and taking advantage of DRIPs, investors can potentially enhance their long-term wealth growth and achieve their financial goals.

It's important to note that not all companies pay dividends, and that investing in dividend-paying companies does not guarantee a profit. Additionally, the amount of the dividend payment may vary from quarter to quarter or year to year, and is subject to change based on the company's financial performance.

When selecting quality dividend-paying stocks for long-term investing, it's important to conduct thorough research and analysis of the company's financial performance, management team, and overall business model. Some factors to consider may include the company's revenue and earnings growth, debt levels, dividend history and payout ratio, and competitive landscape.

Investors should also consider diversifying their portfolio across different sectors and industries to minimize risk and potentially enhance returns. While dividend-paying stocks may offer some degree of stability and consistent income, they should not make up the entirety of an investor's portfolio.

Furthermore, investors should also be aware of the potential tax implications of investing in dividend-paying stocks and DRIPs. Dividend payments may be subject to ordinary income tax rates, and reinvesting dividends through a DRIP may result in taxable gains, even if the investor does not receive any cash payments.

Overall, understanding dividends and DRIPs is an important aspect of long-term investing and can potentially enhance the power of compounding. By conducting thorough research and analysis and working with a financial advisor, investors can make informed investment decisions and achieve their financial goals.

It's worth noting that not all dividend reinvestment plans are created equal, and it's important to carefully evaluate the terms and fees associated with a specific DRIP. Some plans may charge fees for reinvesting dividends or purchasing additional shares, which can eat into potential returns over time.

Additionally, investors should consider the potential opportunity costs of reinvesting dividends through a DRIP versus receiving cash payments and potentially investing those funds elsewhere. Depending on the investor's goals and risk tolerance, it may be more advantageous to receive cash dividends and reinvest them in different assets or use them to pay for living expenses.

Another potential benefit of dividend-paying stocks is their ability to provide a degree of inflation protection. As companies increase their dividend payments over time, the yield on an investor's initial investment may also increase, potentially outpacing the rate of inflation and preserving the purchasing power of their portfolio.

Overall, dividends and DRIPs can be powerful tools for long-term investors seeking to harness the power of compounding. However, it's important to conduct thorough research and analysis, evaluate the potential costs and benefits, and work with a financial advisor to develop a diversified investment strategy that aligns with your financial goals and risk tolerance.

Another important factor to consider when evaluating dividend-paying stocks and DRIPs is the financial health and stability of the underlying companies. Companies with a track record of consistently paying and growing their dividends may be more attractive to long-term investors, as they may have stronger balance sheets, sustainable business models, and a competitive advantage in their respective industries.

On the other hand, companies that are struggling with debt, declining sales, or other financial challenges may be at risk of cutting or suspending their dividend payments, which can have a negative impact on the performance of a dividend-focused portfolio.

Investors should also be mindful of the tax implications of investing in dividend-paying stocks and DRIPs. Dividends are generally subject to federal and state income taxes, and depending on the investor's tax bracket, the tax rate on dividends may be higher than the rate on capital gains.

It's important to remember that investing in individual stocks, including dividend-paying stocks, carries a degree of risk and volatility. To mitigate this risk, investors should consider diversifying their portfolio across different sectors and asset classes, and should work with a financial advisor to develop an investment strategy that aligns with their goals and risk tolerance.

Another potential downside to DRIPs is that they can make it more difficult to rebalance your portfolio. If you have a significant portion of your portfolio tied up in a particular stock or sector, it can be challenging to sell those holdings and reallocate your assets into other areas if needed.

Additionally, DRIPs can be more time-consuming than simply collecting dividend payments and reinvesting them manually. Some investors may prefer the simplicity of cash dividends and the ability to allocate funds as they see fit, rather than being tied to a DRIP plan.

It's important to note that not all companies offer DRIPs, so investors may not have the option to reinvest their dividends in this manner for all their stock holdings. However, many large, well-established companies do offer DRIPs, so there are still plenty of options for investors looking to take advantage of this investment strategy.

Overall, understanding dividends and DRIPs is an important aspect of stock investing for compounding, and investors who are willing to do their due diligence and carefully evaluate their options can potentially reap significant long-term benefits from these strategies.

One key advantage of dividend reinvestment plans is that they can help investors compound their returns over time without incurring additional transaction costs. When dividends are reinvested, they are used to purchase additional shares of the company's stock, which can then generate even more dividends in the future. Over time, this compounding effect can result in significant long-term growth, as the investor's holdings increase in value and generate increasing levels of dividend income.

Another benefit of DRIPs is that they can help investors stay focused on their long-term investment goals. By automatically reinvesting their dividends, investors can avoid the temptation to spend the cash on other things and instead stay committed to their long-term investment strategy. This can be particularly helpful for investors who may be prone to impulsive or emotional decision-making, as DRIPs can help them stay disciplined and focused on their goals.

However, it's important to note that DRIPs are not without their drawbacks. One potential downside is that they can result in fractional shares, which can make it more difficult to manage your portfolio. If you own fractional shares of a company's stock, you may not have the ability to vote in shareholder meetings or participate in certain company events, which could limit your ability to fully participate in the benefits of stock ownership. Additionally, fractional shares may be more difficult to sell, which could impact your ability to quickly liquidate your holdings if needed.

Another potential disadvantage of DRIPs is that they may not be appropriate for all investors. For example, if you rely on your investment income to meet your day-to-day expenses, you may prefer to receive your dividends in cash rather than reinvesting them. Similarly, if you are investing in a stock for the short-term and plan to sell it within a relatively short period of time, DRIPs may not be the best option, as they are geared towards long-term investors who are focused on growth and income over time.

It's also worth noting that not all companies offer DRIPs, and even those that do may have different terms and conditions for their plans. Some may require a minimum investment or limit the number of shares that can be purchased through the plan, while others may charge fees or offer different investment options. As such, it's important to carefully research any DRIP before investing in it, and to consider whether it is appropriate for your investment goals and needs.

While dividend reinvestment plans can be a powerful tool for long-term investors looking to compound their returns, they are not without their drawbacks. It's important to carefully consider the benefits and drawbacks of DRIPs, and to do your due diligence in researching any plan before investing in it. Ultimately, the decision to use a DRIP should be based on your individual investment goals, risk tolerance, and overall financial situation.

Another thing to consider is that while DRIPs can help investors avoid transaction fees, they may still be subject to other costs, such as account maintenance fees, dividend processing fees, and brokerage fees. It's important to carefully review any fees associated with a DRIP and to consider whether they are worth the potential benefits of the plan.

Additionally, investors should be aware that while DRIPs can help to mitigate the effects of market volatility, they are not immune to it. Even high-quality stocks can experience significant price fluctuations, and a DRIP does not protect against losses due to market downturns or company-specific issues.

It's also important to note that DRIPs can have tax implications, as reinvested dividends are generally subject to taxation. Depending on your individual tax situation, it may be more advantageous to receive dividends in cash and then reinvest them on your own, rather than using a DRIP.

Overall, while dividend reinvestment plans can be a powerful tool for long-term investors looking to compound their returns, they are not without their risks and drawbacks. It's important to carefully consider the benefits and drawbacks of DRIPs, and to weigh them against your own investment goals and needs. With careful research and planning, however, DRIPs can be a valuable addition to any investor's portfolio.

CHAPTER *6*

EXAMPLES OF SUCCESSFUL LONG-TERM STOCK INVESTORS

Many successful long-term stock investors share certain characteristics that have contributed to their success. One of the most important is a commitment to a long-term investment strategy that emphasizes patience, discipline, and a focus on quality stocks. These investors are typically not swayed by short-term market fluctuations or the latest investment trends, but instead focus on the fundamentals of individual companies and industries.

Another characteristic of successful long-term investors is their willingness to learn from their mistakes and adapt their strategies as needed. They recognize that investing is a constantly evolving field, and that what worked in the past may not necessarily work in the future. By staying abreast of industry trends and changes, these investors are able to adjust their strategies to changing market conditions and capitalize on new opportunities.

Some examples of successful long-term stock investors include Warren Buffett, Peter Lynch, and John Templeton. Warren Buffett, for example, is known for his value-oriented approach to investing, in which he looks for high-quality companies with strong fundamentals that are trading at a discount to their intrinsic value.

Peter Lynch, on the other hand, was a highly successful mutual fund manager who emphasized the importance of thorough research and analysis when selecting stocks. John Templeton was another renowned investor who was known for his focus on global investing and his ability to identify undervalued companies.

One thing that many people may not know about these successful long-term investors is that they all faced their share of setbacks and challenges along the way. For example, Warren Buffett's Berkshire Hathaway suffered significant losses during the dot-com crash of the early 2000s, while Peter Lynch made some missteps during his tenure at Fidelity Magellan. However, these investors were able to learn from their mistakes and adapt their strategies, ultimately achieving great success over the long term.

Overall, the examples of successful long-term stock investors can provide valuable insights and lessons for investors of all levels. By studying the strategies and approaches of these investors, and by applying them in a thoughtful and disciplined manner, individual investors can work to achieve their own investment goals and build lasting wealth over time.

Many people do not know that successful long-term stock investors have diverse investment strategies and come from a variety of backgrounds. It is not limited to only financial experts or Wall Street professionals. Some of the most successful long-term investors are average individuals who invested in companies they believed in and held onto their shares for a significant period.

One example of a successful long-term investor is Warren Buffett, who is known as one of the most successful investors of all time. He is the chairman and CEO of Berkshire Hathaway and has a net worth of over $100 billion. Buffett has been investing in stocks for over 60 years and has built his wealth through long-term investments in companies that he believed in.

Another example is Peter Lynch, who was the manager of the Fidelity Magellan Fund from 1977 to 1990. Under his leadership, the fund's assets grew from $18 million to $14 billion, and he achieved an annualized return of 29%. Lynch's investment strategy was to invest in companies with strong fundamentals, which had a competitive advantage, and were undervalued.

John Paulson is another example of a successful long-term investor. He is the founder of Paulson & Co., a hedge fund that made a profit of $15 billion during the financial crisis of 2008. Paulson's investment strategy is focused on event-driven opportunities and special situations, such as mergers and acquisitions, bankruptcies, and spin-offs.

These successful investors all have different investment strategies, but they share a commitment to long-term investing and a belief in the power of compounding. They also have a deep understanding of the companies they invest in and are not afraid to hold onto their positions for years or even decades.

One key takeaway from the success stories of long-term stock investors is the importance of patience and discipline. Many successful investors have held their stocks for decades, resisting the temptation to sell during market downturns or fluctuations. They have also followed a well-defined investment strategy and stayed true to their principles, avoiding impulsive decisions based on emotions or short-term market trends.

Another important lesson is the value of diversification. Successful long-term investors have typically held a mix of stocks from different industries and sectors, as well as a balance of domestic and international stocks. This helps to spread out risk and reduce exposure to any one particular market or sector.

Successful long-term investors often have a deep understanding of the companies they invest in, including their financial health, growth potential, and competitive landscape. They have done their homework and conducted thorough research before making investment decisions, allowing them to make informed choices and avoid costly mistakes.

It's also worth noting that successful long-term investors often have a long-term view of the market and the economy. They understand that the stock market can be volatile in the short term, but historically, it has tended to trend upward over longer periods. By taking a patient and disciplined approach, they have been able to weather market downturns and capitalize on long-term growth opportunities.

Another important factor in the success of long-term stock investors is the ability to tune out the noise and focus on the big picture. They understand that there will always be news and events that can affect stock prices in the short term, but they don't let these distractions interfere with their long-term investment strategy. Instead, they stay focused on their goals and remain committed to their long-term investment plan.

Successful long-term stock investors have typically started investing early in life and have been consistent in their investment habits over time. They have taken advantage of the power of compounding by reinvesting their dividends and letting their investments grow over long periods. This has allowed them to accumulate significant wealth and achieve financial independence over time.

Overall, the success stories of long-term stock investors serve as a powerful reminder of the benefits of patience, discipline, and a long-term perspective in investing. While investing in the stock market can be unpredictable and volatile in the short term, by following a well-defined investment strategy and staying focused on the big picture, it is possible to achieve long-term financial success.

PART 3

Bond Investing for Compounding

Chapter 7
Bond Investing for Compounding

Bond investing can be a useful way to diversify your investment portfolio and add stability to your overall investment strategy.

Bonds are essentially loans made by investors to corporations, municipalities, or governments. In exchange for the loan, the issuer of the bond promises to make regular interest payments and to repay the principal amount of the loan at the end of the bond's term.

One of the advantages of bond investing is that it can provide a predictable stream of income through regular interest payments. Unlike stocks, which can be more volatile and offer uncertain returns, bonds are generally considered to be less risky and more stable. This makes them an attractive option for investors who are looking to balance out the riskier elements of their portfolio.

However, there are some important things to consider when investing in bonds. For example, not all bonds are created equal. Some bonds are riskier than others, depending on the creditworthiness of the issuer. Investors should carefully evaluate the credit ratings of the issuers of the bonds they are considering, as well as the terms of the bond, including the interest rate and maturity date.

In addition, bond investing requires a longer-term investment horizon in order to benefit from the power of compounding. This is because the interest earned on a bond investment is typically fixed, and does not compound over time in the same way that stock investments can. However, investors can still benefit from compounding by reinvesting the interest payments they receive from their bond investments.

Another factor to consider when investing in bonds is the impact of inflation on the value of the investment. Inflation can erode the value of the interest payments received from bonds over time, particularly if the interest rate on the bond is lower than the rate of inflation.

Overall, bond investing can be an effective strategy for compounding wealth over the long term, particularly for investors who are looking for stability and predictable income from their investments. However, it is important to carefully evaluate the creditworthiness of the issuer and the terms of the bond, and to have a long-term investment horizon in order to benefit from the power of compounding.

Bond investing can be a useful way to diversify a portfolio and reduce overall risk. While stocks can be volatile and unpredictable, bonds are generally more stable and reliable. They can provide a steady income stream through interest payments and can help offset any losses in the stock market.

There are many different types of bonds, including government bonds, corporate bonds, municipal bonds, and more. Each type of bond has its own unique characteristics, risks, and potential rewards. It's important to understand the differences between these types of bonds before making any investment decisions.

One important metric to consider when evaluating bonds is their credit rating. Bonds are rated by independent agencies like Moody's and Standard & Poor's, based on the likelihood of the issuer defaulting on its debt. Bonds with higher credit ratings are generally considered safer and more reliable, but they may also offer lower yields.

Like stocks, bond prices can fluctuate over time in response to changing market conditions. However, bonds are generally less volatile than stocks and may be less affected by short-term market fluctuations. As a result, bond investing may be more suitable for investors with a lower tolerance for risk.

When investing in bonds for compounding, it's important to consider the time horizon of the investment. Long-term bonds typically offer higher yields than short-term bonds, but they also carry more risk. Investors should carefully evaluate their investment goals and risk tolerance before making any decisions.

One popular way to invest in bonds is through bond funds or exchange-traded funds (ETFs). These funds allow investors to gain exposure to a diversified portfolio of bonds with relatively low fees and minimal effort. However, investors should carefully review the fees and underlying holdings of any bond fund before making an investment.

Finally, it's worth noting that bond investing for compounding may not be suitable for all investors. As with any investment strategy, there is no guarantee of returns, and there is always some risk involved. It's important to do your own research and consult with a financial advisor before making any investment decisions.

Certainly! When investing in bonds, it's important to understand the different types of bonds available. Many people may not realize that there are several types of bonds to choose from, including government bonds, corporate bonds, municipal bonds, and international bonds.

Government bonds are issued by the government and are generally considered the safest type of bond since they are backed by the full faith and credit of the government. Corporate bonds, on the other hand, are issued by corporations and are considered riskier than government bonds since they are not backed by a government guarantee.

Municipal bonds are issued by local governments, such as cities or states, and are typically used to fund infrastructure projects. They are generally exempt from federal taxes and sometimes state and local taxes, making them a popular choice for investors seeking tax-free income.

International bonds are issued by foreign governments or corporations and can be denominated in a variety of currencies. These bonds can offer higher yields than domestic bonds but also come with additional risks, such as currency fluctuations and political instability.

Another important aspect of bond investing is understanding the concept of credit ratings. Credit rating agencies like Standard & Poor's and Moody's provide ratings for bonds based on the creditworthiness of the issuer. Bonds with higher credit ratings are generally considered less risky than those with lower ratings, but they also tend to offer lower yields.

Finally, it's important to understand the relationship between bond prices and interest rates. When interest rates rise, bond prices typically fall, and when interest rates fall, bond prices typically rise. This can have a significant impact on the value of a bond portfolio, especially for long-term bond investors.

Introduction to bonds and bond investing

Bonds are a type of fixed-income investment that are commonly used by individuals, corporations, and governments to raise capital. When an investor buys a bond, they are essentially lending money to the issuer of the bond in exchange for regular interest payments and the return of their principal investment at the bond's maturity.

One important thing that many people may not know about bonds is that they have a lower risk profile than stocks, making them a popular choice for more conservative investors. However, this lower risk is typically accompanied by lower returns than the potential returns of stocks.

Another important aspect of bond investing that is often overlooked is the impact of interest rates on bond prices. As interest rates rise, bond prices tend to fall, and vice versa. This means that it's important to pay attention to interest rate trends when investing in bonds, as they can have a significant impact on the value of your bond holdings.

In addition, there are several types of bonds, including government bonds, municipal bonds, and corporate bonds, each with their own unique characteristics and risks. It's important to understand the differences between these types of bonds and how they fit into your overall investment strategy.

Investors can also choose between individual bonds and bond funds. While individual bonds offer the potential for more stable returns, they require a larger initial investment and may be less diversified than bond funds. Bond funds, on the other hand, offer greater diversification and typically have lower initial investment requirements, but may have higher management fees.

Overall, bonds can be a valuable component of a long-term investment strategy, offering diversification and potentially lower risk compared to stocks. However, it's important to understand the risks and characteristics of bonds and how they fit into your overall investment portfolio.

Many people may not realize that bonds can be a great addition to a well-diversified investment portfolio. Bonds are essentially a type of loan that you give to a company or government. In exchange, the issuer of the bond agrees to pay you interest at regular intervals (usually annually or semi-annually) and to repay the full amount of the loan (the face value of the bond) at a specified date in the future.

One important characteristic of bonds is that they are generally considered to be less risky than stocks. This is because the interest and principal payments on bonds are typically more predictable than the earnings of stocks. In addition, in the event of bankruptcy, bondholders are usually paid before stockholders.

Bonds can also offer higher yields than savings accounts and other low-risk investments. However, it is important to remember that bonds do carry some risk. For example, if interest rates rise, the value of existing bonds may decline, as new bonds issued with higher yields become more attractive to investors. It is also possible for the issuer of a bond to default, which can result in a loss of principal.

Despite these risks, many investors choose to include bonds in their portfolios as a way to balance out the higher risk of stocks and potentially generate income.

One of the key benefits of bond investing is the relatively lower risk compared to stocks. While bonds are not completely risk-free, they are generally considered less risky than stocks, as they provide regular interest payments and have a set maturity date.

When investing in bonds, it's important to consider the credit quality of the issuer. Bonds issued by higher-quality companies or governments are generally considered less risky than those issued by lower-quality or high-yield companies.

There are different types of bonds available for investors, including government bonds, corporate bonds, municipal bonds, and international bonds. Each type of bond comes with its own set of risks and rewards, and it's important to understand these before investing.

Bond prices and interest rates are inversely related, meaning that when interest rates rise, bond prices generally fall, and vice versa. This is an important factor to consider when investing in bonds, as rising interest rates can lead to a decrease in the value of your bond investments.

Bond mutual funds and exchange-traded funds (ETFs) can be a good way for individual investors to gain exposure to a diversified portfolio of bonds. These funds are managed by professional investment managers and can provide investors with greater diversification than individual bond investments. However, they also come with management fees and expenses that should be considered.

Finally, it's important to have a long-term investment horizon when investing in bonds, as compounding returns over time can help to maximize the benefits of this investment strategy. By reinvesting interest payments and holding bonds to maturity, investors can achieve a steady stream of income and potential capital gains.

CHAPTER *8*

THE DIFFERENT TYPES OF BONDS AND THEIR RISKS

When it comes to bond investing, it's important to understand the different types of bonds and the risks associated with them. Here are some things many people may not know about this topic:

Government bonds: These are issued by governments and are generally considered to be the safest type of bond. They are backed by the government's ability to tax its citizens, and they typically offer lower yields compared to other types of bonds.

Municipal bonds: These are issued by state and local governments to finance public projects such as schools, hospitals, and highways. They are exempt from federal taxes and may be exempt from state and local taxes, making them attractive to investors in higher tax brackets. However, municipal bonds are not risk-free, and their creditworthiness can vary depending on the financial health of the issuer.

Corporate bonds: These are issued by corporations to raise capital for business purposes. They are generally riskier than government bonds and municipal bonds because the creditworthiness of the issuer is tied to the success of the company. Corporate bonds can be further classified into investment-grade and high-yield (also known as junk) bonds.

International bonds: These are issued by foreign governments and corporations, and they come with additional risks such as currency risk and political risk.

It's important to understand the risks associated with each type of bond and to diversify your bond portfolio to mitigate risk. In addition to credit risk, there is also interest rate risk, which is the risk that interest rates will rise and cause the value of the bond to decline. Bond investing can be complex, but with proper research and diversification, it can be a valuable component of a long-term investment strategy.

Municipal bonds: Municipal bonds are issued by state and local governments to fund public projects like schools, highways, and hospitals. They are generally considered to be low-risk, as the likelihood of default is low due to the government's ability to raise revenue through taxes. However, there is some risk involved in municipal bonds, particularly those issued by smaller or less financially stable municipalities.

Corporate bonds: Corporate bonds are issued by companies to fund their operations or investments. They are generally riskier than government bonds, as the likelihood of default is higher. The risk of default depends on the financial health of the company issuing the bond, with companies with lower credit ratings carrying a higher risk.

High-yield bonds: High-yield bonds, also known as junk bonds, are issued by companies with lower credit ratings and a higher risk of default. They offer higher yields to compensate for the increased risk, making them attractive to investors seeking higher returns. However, they also carry a higher risk of default, which means investors can lose their principal.

Treasury bonds: Treasury bonds are issued by the U.S. government to fund its operations. They are considered to be among the safest investments, as they are backed by the full faith and credit of the U.S. government. However, like all investments, they carry some risk, particularly in the form of inflation risk.

International bonds: International bonds are issued by foreign governments or companies, and can offer higher yields than U.S. bonds. However, they also carry additional risks, such as currency risk and political risk.

Inflation-protected bonds: Inflation-protected bonds, also known as TIPS (Treasury Inflation-Protected Securities), are issued by the U.S. government and offer protection against inflation. The principal of the bond is adjusted for inflation, meaning that the value of the investment increases as inflation rises. While TIPS are considered to be low-risk, they do carry some risk, particularly in the form of interest rate risk.

It's important to note that there are many other types of bonds available, and that the risks and rewards of investing in bonds can vary widely depending on the specifics of the investment. It's important to do your research and understand the risks before investing in any bond.

Government bonds: Government bonds are generally considered to be the safest type of bond because they are backed by the full faith and credit of the government. However, there is still some risk involved as there is always the possibility that a government may default on its bonds.

Corporate bonds: Corporate bonds are issued by companies and come with a higher degree of risk than government bonds. The risk associated with corporate bonds depends on the financial health of the company issuing the bond. If the company experiences financial difficulties or goes bankrupt, bondholders may not receive the full value of their investment.

Municipal bonds: Municipal bonds are issued by state and local governments to finance public projects such as roads, schools, and hospitals. These bonds generally offer tax benefits to investors, but they can also carry some risk. The risk associated with municipal bonds depends on the financial health of the issuing government, as well as the project being financed.

High-yield bonds: High-yield bonds, also known as junk bonds, are issued by companies with a lower credit rating, and they carry a higher degree of risk than other types of bonds. The higher risk is reflected in the higher yield offered to investors.

Foreign bonds: Foreign bonds are issued by governments or companies in other countries, and they carry additional risks such as currency risk and political risk. Currency risk refers to the risk that the exchange rate between the foreign currency and the investor's home currency will change, reducing the value of the investment. Political risk refers to the risk that the government or economic conditions in the foreign country will change, affecting the value of the investment.

It is important to understand the risks associated with different types of bonds before investing, and to consider the potential returns in relation to those risks. Investors should also diversify their bond investments to spread risk across different types of bonds and issuers.

Strategies for using bonds in a compounding portfolio

When it comes to using bonds in a compounding portfolio, there are a few strategies that investors can use to maximize their returns while minimizing their risk. Here are some things that many people may not know about these strategies:

Diversification is key: One of the most important strategies for using bonds in a compounding portfolio is diversification. Investors should not only invest in different types of bonds but also in different sectors and industries. This helps to spread the risk and minimize the impact of any single bond defaulting.

Consider bond funds: Bond funds can provide an easy and convenient way to invest in a diversified portfolio of bonds. These funds are managed by professional fund managers who specialize in bond investing and can provide expertise in selecting the right bonds to invest in.

Use bond ladders: Another strategy for using bonds in a compounding portfolio is to use bond ladders. A bond ladder is a portfolio of bonds that mature at different times. This allows investors to take advantage of higher interest rates on longer-term bonds while still maintaining liquidity and reducing interest rate risk.

Be aware of interest rate risk: One of the main risks associated with bond investing is interest rate risk. As interest rates rise, the value of existing bonds will fall. Investors can mitigate this risk by investing in bonds with shorter maturities, which are less sensitive to interest rate changes, or by using a bond ladder.

Monitor credit risk: Bond investors should also be aware of credit risk, which is the risk that the issuer will default on the bond. It's important to monitor the creditworthiness of the issuer and to invest in bonds with a high credit rating to minimize this risk.

By using these strategies, investors can make the most of their bond investments and build a diversified portfolio that can generate steady returns over the long term.

Another strategy for using bonds in a compounding portfolio is to use a bond ladder. This involves purchasing multiple bonds that have staggered maturity dates, such that the bonds mature at regular intervals. By doing this, an investor can ensure that they have a steady stream of income from the interest payments, as well as a regular supply of cash from the maturing bonds. The investor can then reinvest the cash from the maturing bonds into new bonds with longer maturities, thereby continuing the cycle of compound growth.

Another strategy is to use bond funds or ETFs (exchange-traded funds), which offer diversification and professional management. Bond funds and ETFs pool the resources of many investors to purchase a portfolio of bonds, which can provide greater diversification and potentially lower risk than purchasing individual bonds. These funds may also offer the benefit of reinvesting interest payments automatically, which can help to compound returns over time.

It's also important to consider the tax implications of investing in bonds. Interest income from bonds is typically taxable at the federal and state levels, so investors may want to consider investing in tax-free municipal bonds, which are issued by state and local governments and are typically exempt from federal taxes. However, it's important to note that these bonds may carry a higher risk than other types of bonds.

Overall, investing in bonds can be an important part of a compounding portfolio, providing a source of income and helping to diversify risk. It's important to consider the different types of bonds and their risks, as well as various strategies for using bonds in a portfolio, in order to make informed investment decisions.

How to reinvest bond income for maximum growth

Reinvesting bond income can be an effective strategy for maximizing growth in a compounding portfolio. When investors receive coupon payments from their bonds, they have the option to reinvest the income back into the bond or into other investments.

One strategy for reinvesting bond income is to use a bond ladder. A bond ladder involves investing in bonds with different maturities, so that the bonds mature at staggered intervals. As each bond matures, the investor can reinvest the proceeds into another bond with a longer maturity, potentially earning a higher yield. This strategy can provide a steady stream of income and reduce the risk of interest rate fluctuations.

Another strategy for reinvesting bond income is to use a bond mutual fund or exchange-traded fund (ETF). These funds invest in a diversified portfolio of bonds and can provide regular income through distributions. When these distributions are reinvested, they can help compound the growth of the portfolio.

Many investors may not be aware that they can reinvest bond income into stocks or other investments for potentially higher returns. This can be done by selling the bonds and using the proceeds to purchase other investments, or by using a dividend reinvestment plan (DRIP) offered by some companies. DRIPs allow investors to reinvest their dividend payments into additional shares of the company's stock, potentially compounding the growth of their investment.

It's important to note that there are risks associated with reinvesting bond income, and investors should carefully consider their goals and risk tolerance before implementing any strategy. Additionally, taxes can also affect the total return of a bond investment, so it's important to consult with a financial advisor or tax professional for guidance on how to maximize the potential benefits of reinvesting bond income.

One strategy for maximizing growth through bond income reinvestment is to consider using a bond ladder. A bond ladder is a portfolio of bonds with varying maturities that can help manage risk and provide a regular income stream. With a bond ladder, an investor can stagger the maturity dates of their bonds to match their income needs or investment goals.

For example, an investor might build a bond ladder with bonds maturing in 1, 3, 5, and 7 years. As each bond matures, the investor can reinvest the principal into a new bond with the longest maturity in the ladder. This allows the investor to maintain a constant stream of income while also benefiting from the potential for higher returns with longer-term bonds.

Another strategy is to reinvest bond income into a bond mutual fund or ETF. This allows for diversification and professional management, as the fund's portfolio manager will actively manage the portfolio to try to generate the highest returns for investors.

It's also important to consider the tax implications of reinvesting bond income. Some bond funds distribute income monthly or quarterly, which can result in taxable income. However, reinvesting bond income within a tax-advantaged retirement account can help to minimize tax liabilities and maximize growth potential.

Overall, reinvesting bond income is a key component of a successful compounding portfolio. By utilizing strategies such as bond ladders and mutual funds or ETFs, investors can maximize growth potential and manage risk over the long term.

PART 4

Cryptocurrency Investing for Compounding

CHAPTER *9*

CRYPTOCURRENCY INVESTING FOR COMPOUNDING

Cryptocurrency investing has become increasingly popular in recent years, and for good reason. While it may seem like a new and risky investment option, many investors have found that cryptocurrency has the potential for high returns when used as a long-term investment strategy. However, there are several things that many people do not know about cryptocurrency investing that can help ensure their success in the long run.

First, it is important to understand the basics of cryptocurrency. Unlike traditional currency, cryptocurrency is decentralized and operates through a network of computers rather than a central authority. This means that the value of a cryptocurrency, such as Bitcoin or Ethereum, is based on supply and demand in the market. Cryptocurrencies are typically traded on exchanges, where buyers and sellers can exchange them for other currencies or goods and services.

One important thing to keep in mind when investing in cryptocurrency is the volatility of the market. Cryptocurrencies are known for their price fluctuations, and it is not uncommon to see significant swings in value over a short period of time. This can make it difficult to predict market trends and can be a major source of risk for investors. However, many experts believe that this volatility is a natural part of the growth and development of the cryptocurrency market, and that over time it will stabilize and become less volatile.

Another important factor to consider when investing in cryptocurrency is the security of your investments. Since cryptocurrencies operate through a decentralized network, they are vulnerable to hacking and other cyber attacks. To protect your investments, it is important to use secure storage options such as cold wallets, and to always use strong passwords and two-factor authentication when logging into your cryptocurrency accounts.

Finally, it is important to have a long-term perspective when investing in cryptocurrency. While it may be tempting to try to time the market and buy and sell quickly, the most successful cryptocurrency investors have taken a long-term approach, buying and holding their investments over time. This allows them to benefit from the power of compounding, which can lead to significant returns over the long run.

Overall, cryptocurrency investing can be a powerful tool for compounding wealth, but it is important to have a deep understanding of the market and the risks involved before making any investment decisions. With the right approach, however, cryptocurrency investing can be a lucrative and exciting addition to any investment portfolio.

Cryptocurrency has been gaining popularity as an investment option for compounding over the past few years. While many people see it as a volatile and risky investment, there are ways to approach cryptocurrency investing that can help mitigate those risks and maximize returns.

One thing that many people may not know is that there are hundreds of different cryptocurrencies available to invest in, each with their own unique features and potential benefits. Some of the most popular cryptocurrencies include Bitcoin, Ethereum, Litecoin, and Ripple, but there are many others that may be worth considering as well.

Another important factor to consider when investing in cryptocurrencies is the concept of blockchain technology, which underlies the functioning of most cryptocurrencies. Blockchain is a decentralized digital ledger that keeps track of all transactions made using a particular cryptocurrency. This technology has the potential to revolutionize many industries, and some investors believe that investing in cryptocurrencies that utilize blockchain technology could be a smart long-term play.

Additionally, many people may not be aware of the risks associated with cryptocurrency investing, such as volatility, regulation, and security concerns. Because cryptocurrencies are relatively new and not yet widely regulated, the value of a particular cryptocurrency can fluctuate wildly over short periods of time, and there is always the possibility of fraud or theft.

To mitigate these risks, some strategies that investors use include investing in a diverse range of cryptocurrencies to spread out risk, setting stop-loss orders to automatically sell when prices drop to a certain level, and keeping their investments in secure cold wallets rather than on exchanges where they could be more vulnerable to hacking.

Overall, while cryptocurrency investing for compounding can be a complex and risky process, with proper research and risk management, it could potentially offer strong returns over the long term.

When it comes to cryptocurrency investing for compounding, it is important to understand the unique risks and opportunities involved. One thing many people do not know is that the cryptocurrency market can be highly volatile, with prices often experiencing rapid and extreme fluctuations. This means that while it is possible to achieve high returns through cryptocurrency investing, it is also possible to experience significant losses.

Another thing to consider is that the cryptocurrency market is still relatively new and there is a lot of uncertainty around future regulations and market trends. Additionally, not all cryptocurrencies are created equal, and some are riskier or more speculative than others. It is important to do thorough research and due diligence before investing in any particular cryptocurrency.

That being said, there are also many potential benefits to investing in cryptocurrencies for compounding. One of the main advantages is the potential for high returns, as the market has historically experienced rapid growth. Additionally, cryptocurrencies are not tied to traditional financial systems and can offer unique diversification benefits to a portfolio.

When it comes to investing in cryptocurrencies for compounding, it is important to have a clear investment strategy and to be prepared for potential risks and losses. It is also important to use a reputable cryptocurrency exchange and to keep your cryptocurrency investments secure through proper storage and security measures. Finally, diversification is key, and it is important to consider investing in a range of different cryptocurrencies to spread out risk and maximize potential returns.

Introduction to cryptocurrencies

Cryptocurrency is a digital or virtual currency that uses cryptography for security and operates independently of a central bank. It is decentralized, meaning that it is not subject to government control, and it relies on a distributed ledger technology called the blockchain to record and verify transactions. Cryptocurrencies are often traded on specialized online platforms, and their value can be highly volatile, fluctuating significantly over short periods.

One thing that many people may not know about cryptocurrencies is that they were initially designed to function as a means of exchange, rather than an investment vehicle. The first cryptocurrency, Bitcoin, was created in 2009 as a way for people to transfer money electronically without the need for a centralized intermediary such as a bank. Since then, many other cryptocurrencies have been developed, each with its own unique characteristics and uses.

Cryptocurrencies have become increasingly popular in recent years, with many investors buying them as a speculative investment. However, it's important to note that cryptocurrencies can be risky, and their values can fluctuate widely in short periods of time. Additionally, the regulatory landscape for cryptocurrencies is constantly evolving, which can create uncertainty for investors.

It's also worth noting that the use of cryptocurrencies in everyday transactions is still relatively limited, and their adoption as a mainstream currency is not yet widespread. While some businesses accept cryptocurrencies as payment, many do not, and their use as a medium of exchange is still somewhat niche. Despite this, the potential for blockchain technology to disrupt traditional industries and create new opportunities is significant, and many believe that cryptocurrencies will play a significant role in the future of finance.

Cryptocurrencies are decentralized: Unlike traditional currencies that are backed by governments, cryptocurrencies are decentralized and operate on a peer-to-peer network. This means that there is no central authority controlling them, and transactions are verified and recorded by a network of users rather than a central authority.

Cryptocurrencies are highly volatile: The value of cryptocurrencies can fluctuate rapidly and dramatically, sometimes within hours or even minutes. This volatility is due to a variety of factors, including changes in public sentiment, regulatory changes, and technological advancements.

There are many different cryptocurrencies: Bitcoin is the most well-known and valuable cryptocurrency, but there are hundreds of others, each with its unique features and functions.

Cryptocurrencies are highly secure: Cryptocurrencies use advanced encryption and security protocols to ensure that transactions are secure and that the integrity of the blockchain is maintained.

Cryptocurrencies can be bought and sold on exchanges: Just like stocks or other traditional investments, cryptocurrencies can be bought and sold on specialized exchanges. These exchanges typically charge a fee for each transaction.

Cryptocurrencies are not accepted everywhere: While the number of merchants and businesses accepting cryptocurrencies is increasing, they are still not widely accepted as a form of payment. This means that cryptocurrencies are still primarily used as an investment rather than a means of exchange.

Cryptocurrencies can be stored in digital wallets: Cryptocurrencies are stored in digital wallets, which can be either hot or cold. Hot wallets are connected to the internet and are generally more convenient for everyday use, while cold wallets are offline and offer a higher level of security for long-term storage.

Overall, cryptocurrencies are a complex and rapidly evolving asset class that requires a deep understanding of technology and economics to invest in successfully. As with any investment, it is important to do your research, understand the risks involved, and invest only what you can afford to lose.

Cryptocurrencies are decentralized: Unlike traditional currencies, which are managed by central authorities, cryptocurrencies are decentralized. This means that no government or financial institution has control over them, and they operate independently of any central authority.

Cryptocurrencies are not physical: Unlike traditional currencies, cryptocurrencies are entirely digital and exist only as entries on a digital ledger called a blockchain.

Cryptocurrencies are not anonymous: While cryptocurrencies are often associated with anonymity, most cryptocurrencies are actually pseudonymous. This means that transactions are recorded on the blockchain and can be traced back to the users who made them.

Cryptocurrencies are volatile: The value of cryptocurrencies can fluctuate rapidly and dramatically, making them a high-risk investment.

There are thousands of cryptocurrencies: While Bitcoin is the most well-known cryptocurrency, there are thousands of other cryptocurrencies available for investment, each with its own unique features and potential risks and rewards.

Cryptocurrency markets are open 24/7: Unlike traditional stock markets, which have set trading hours, cryptocurrency markets are open 24 hours a day, 7 days a week.

Cryptocurrencies are not universally accepted: While many businesses and individuals now accept cryptocurrencies as payment, they are not yet universally accepted, and their use is still relatively limited compared to traditional currencies.

Cryptocurrency regulation is still developing: As cryptocurrencies are relatively new, there is still a lot of uncertainty surrounding how they will be regulated. Different countries have different approaches to cryptocurrency regulation, and it is important for investors to stay informed about the latest developments.

PART 5
THE POTENTIAL FOR GROWTH AND RISK IN CRYPTOCURRENCY INVESTING

CHAPTER *10*

THE POTENTIAL FOR GROWTH AND RISK IN CRYPTOCURRENCY INVESTING

Cryptocurrency investing has the potential for significant growth and returns, but it also carries high risks. The cryptocurrency market is highly volatile and unpredictable, and prices can fluctuate rapidly and dramatically. It is not uncommon to see price swings of 20% or more in a single day.

One of the main risks of investing in cryptocurrency is the lack of regulation and security. Cryptocurrencies are not backed by any government or financial institution, and there is no FDIC insurance for them. This makes them susceptible to fraud, hacking, and other security breaches.

Another risk is the lack of transparency in the cryptocurrency market. Because cryptocurrencies are decentralized and unregulated, there is often limited information available about the underlying technology and the companies or individuals behind them. This makes it difficult to evaluate the long-term prospects of a particular cryptocurrency and assess its true value.

However, despite these risks, the potential for growth in the cryptocurrency market is significant. Bitcoin, the first and most well-known cryptocurrency, has seen tremendous growth in value since its creation in 2009. While its value has experienced significant fluctuations, it has also seen dramatic gains, with some early investors seeing returns of over 1000%.

Other cryptocurrencies, such as Ethereum, Ripple, and Litecoin, have also seen significant growth in recent years. Many investors believe that the potential for growth in the cryptocurrency market is still significant, and that it may be a good option for those willing to take on the risks involved.

Overall, it is important for investors to thoroughly research the risks and potential rewards of cryptocurrency investing before making any investment decisions. They should also consider their risk tolerance and overall investment strategy before investing in cryptocurrencies.

Another thing that many people do not know about the potential for growth and risk in cryptocurrency investing is the impact of regulations and government actions. Cryptocurrencies have faced increasing scrutiny and regulation from governments around the world. Some governments have banned or severely restricted the use of cryptocurrencies, while others have embraced them.

In addition to government regulation, there are other risks associated with cryptocurrency investing that investors should be aware of. For example, cryptocurrencies are highly volatile and can experience significant price fluctuations in a short period of time. This volatility can be driven by a variety of factors, including market speculation, news events, and changes in the regulatory environment.

Another risk associated with cryptocurrency investing is the potential for fraud and hacking. Cryptocurrencies are decentralized and operate on a peer-to-peer network, which makes them vulnerable to cyber attacks and fraud. Investors need to be cautious and take steps to secure their investments, such as using reputable exchanges and wallets and maintaining strong passwords.

Despite these risks, many investors are drawn to cryptocurrencies because of their potential for growth. Cryptocurrencies have experienced rapid price increases in the past, and some investors believe that they have the potential to disrupt traditional financial systems and become widely adopted in the future. However, as with any investment, it is important to carefully consider the risks and potential rewards before investing in cryptocurrencies.

Certainly! One thing that many people may not realize about the risks of cryptocurrency investing is the potential for extreme volatility. Unlike traditional investments such as stocks and bonds, the value of cryptocurrencies can fluctuate dramatically in a short period of time. For example, the value of Bitcoin, the most well-known cryptocurrency, has experienced significant fluctuations in recent years, from a high of nearly $20,000 in late 2017 to a low of around $3,000 in early 2019, before rising again to over $60,000 in early 2021.

Additionally, the lack of regulation and oversight in the cryptocurrency market can make it vulnerable to fraud and other types of illegal activities. There have been numerous instances of cryptocurrency exchanges being hacked or going bankrupt, resulting in the loss of investor funds.

Furthermore, some countries have imposed restrictions or outright bans on cryptocurrency trading, which can limit the potential for growth in certain markets.

It is important for investors to carefully consider these and other risks before investing in cryptocurrency, and to approach this type of investing with caution and a solid understanding of the technology and market.

Strategies for investing in cryptocurrencies for the long-term

Investing in cryptocurrencies can be a highly speculative and volatile endeavor, with the potential for significant gains or losses. However, for those willing to take the risk, there are a few strategies to consider when investing in cryptocurrencies for the long-term.

Diversification: Diversifying your portfolio is a basic investment principle that is as relevant for cryptocurrencies as it is for any other asset class. By investing in a range of different cryptocurrencies, you can reduce your overall risk exposure, as the performance of one coin is unlikely to significantly impact your entire portfolio.

Dollar-cost averaging: Dollar-cost averaging is a strategy where you invest a fixed amount of money in regular intervals, regardless of the current price of the asset. This can be a helpful way to mitigate the risk of volatility in the cryptocurrency market, as it allows you to buy more coins when prices are low and fewer coins when prices are high.

Research and analysis: Investing in cryptocurrencies requires a thorough understanding of the technology and underlying fundamentals of each coin. Before investing, conduct thorough research on the projects, development teams, partnerships, and use cases of the coins you are interested in. Additionally, keep up-to-date with the latest news and trends in the cryptocurrency market, as it can have a significant impact on the prices of individual coins.

HODL: HODL is a term in the cryptocurrency community that stands for "hold on for dear life." This means that rather than panic selling during periods of market volatility, you hold onto your coins for the long-term, as the cryptocurrency market has historically seen significant growth over time. However, it is important to note that HODLing does not mean ignoring market conditions altogether, and investors should always keep an eye on the market and adjust their strategies accordingly.

Hardware wallet: Cryptocurrencies are stored in digital wallets, which can be susceptible to hacking and theft. To mitigate this risk, consider investing in a hardware wallet, which is a physical device that stores your coins offline. This can provide an added layer of security and protect your coins from potential cyber threats.

It is important to note that investing in cryptocurrencies carries significant risks, and investors should only invest what they can afford to lose. Additionally, it is always wise to consult with a financial advisor before making any investment decisions.

One important aspect of long-term cryptocurrency investing is diversification. Since the cryptocurrency market is highly volatile and unpredictable, investing in a single cryptocurrency could be risky. Therefore, investors should consider spreading their investments across multiple cryptocurrencies, preferably ones with different use cases, market capitalizations, and risk profiles. By diversifying, investors can potentially reduce their exposure to market risks and benefit from the overall growth of the cryptocurrency market.

Another strategy for long-term cryptocurrency investing is to practice dollar-cost averaging. This involves investing a fixed amount of money into a chosen cryptocurrency on a regular basis, regardless of its market value. By buying at different market prices over time, investors can potentially benefit from the average cost of their investment and avoid the volatility of the market.

Furthermore, investors should consider taking a long-term perspective and avoiding the temptation to make short-term trades based on market volatility. Cryptocurrency investing requires patience and a willingness to hold onto investments for an extended period, regardless of temporary price fluctuations. Investors who take a long-term approach and believe in the potential of the technology behind the cryptocurrencies they invest in are more likely to see their investments grow over time.

Finally, investors should carefully research and analyze the cryptocurrencies they are considering investing in. This involves understanding the technology, the market demand, the competition, and any regulatory risks that could affect the cryptocurrency's value. By conducting thorough research and analysis, investors can make informed decisions and potentially minimize the risks of investing in cryptocurrencies.

Chapter 11
EXAMPLES OF SUCCESSFUL CRYPTOCURRENCY INVESTORS

Cryptocurrency has been a popular investment choice for many individuals due to its potential for high returns. Some investors have been incredibly successful in their cryptocurrency investments and have made millions of dollars in profits.

One of the most famous examples of a successful cryptocurrency investor is the Winklevoss twins, who are known for their early investment in Bitcoin. In 2013, the Winklevoss twins invested $11 million in Bitcoin, which was worth around $120 at the time. As of February 2023, the value of their Bitcoin holdings has increased to over $1.2 billion.

Another example of a successful cryptocurrency investor is Michael Saylor, the CEO of MicroStrategy, a business intelligence company. Saylor has been a vocal advocate for Bitcoin and has invested heavily in the cryptocurrency. In 2020, his company purchased over $1 billion worth of Bitcoin, which has since increased significantly in value. As of February 2023, MicroStrategy's Bitcoin holdings are worth over $10 billion.

However, it is important to note that the cryptocurrency market is highly volatile and unpredictable. While there have been successful investors, there have also been individuals who have lost large sums of money in their cryptocurrency investments. It is crucial to thoroughly research and understand the risks before making any investments in cryptocurrencies. Additionally, it is recommended to diversify your investment portfolio and not to allocate all your funds to one asset class.

While there are many successful cryptocurrency investors, it is important to note that their success may not necessarily translate to others who attempt to replicate their strategies. It is crucial to do your own research and invest with caution, as the cryptocurrency market is notoriously volatile and unpredictable. Additionally, some of the most successful cryptocurrency investors have been involved in the industry for years, with a deep understanding of the technology and its potential. It is important to keep this in mind and not expect overnight success.

One key example of a successful cryptocurrency investor is the Winklevoss twins, who famously sued Mark Zuckerberg over the creation of Facebook. After settling the lawsuit, the twins used the money they received to invest in Bitcoin in 2012, when the currency was still in its early stages. Since then, they have been strong advocates for the cryptocurrency industry and have made several successful investments in the space.

Another notable example is Barry Silbert, the founder of Digital Currency Group, a venture capital firm that focuses on blockchain and cryptocurrency companies. Silbert has been involved in the industry since 2012 and has invested in a number of successful companies, including Coinbase and Ripple. He is also the creator of the Grayscale Bitcoin Trust, which allows investors to gain exposure to Bitcoin without actually owning the cryptocurrency.

While these individuals have found success in the cryptocurrency market, it is important to remember that every investor's experience is different, and that past performance is not a guarantee of future results. It is important to do your own research, diversify your portfolio, and invest with caution in any asset, including cryptocurrencies.

I apologize for the previous message, here are some additional points on the topic of "Examples of successful cryptocurrency investors" that you may find useful:

One example of a successful cryptocurrency investor is Tyler and Cameron Winklevoss, who are known for their early investment in Bitcoin. The twins reportedly invested $11 million in Bitcoin in 2013, which was worth over $1 billion by the end of 2017. They have since founded the cryptocurrency exchange Gemini and have continued to advocate for the adoption of Bitcoin and other cryptocurrencies.

Another successful cryptocurrency investor is Michael Novogratz, a former hedge fund manager who founded Galaxy Digital, a full-service cryptocurrency merchant bank. Novogratz has been a strong advocate for Bitcoin and other cryptocurrencies, and has made several successful investments in the industry. He has also been a vocal critic of traditional financial institutions and has predicted that cryptocurrencies will eventually replace traditional currencies.

Barry Silbert, the founder and CEO of Digital Currency Group, is another example of a successful cryptocurrency investor. Silbert has been a vocal supporter of Bitcoin and has invested in several successful cryptocurrency startups, including Coinbase and BitPay. He has also been involved in the creation of several cryptocurrency investment funds, including the Bitcoin Investment Trust and the Ethereum Classic Investment Trust.

Finally, Roger Ver, also known as "Bitcoin Jesus," is a successful cryptocurrency investor and early adopter of Bitcoin. Ver has been involved in the industry since its early days and has invested in several successful Bitcoin-related startups. He is also a vocal advocate for the use of cryptocurrencies as a means of achieving greater financial freedom and has been involved in several high-profile debates and controversies within the industry.

PART 6
MAXIMIZING THE POWER OF COMPOUNDING

CHAPTER *12*

MAXIMIZING THE POWER OF COMPOUNDING

Compounding is a powerful financial concept that is often overlooked or misunderstood by many people. The power of compounding is the ability to generate earnings on both the principal amount invested and the interest or earnings generated from that investment over time. By reinvesting the earnings, investors can generate exponential growth in their portfolios, which is especially important for long-term investors.

One of the things many people do not know about compounding is the impact of fees on investment returns. Fees, including management fees, transaction fees, and other expenses, can significantly reduce the overall return on an investment, which in turn reduces the power of compounding. It is crucial for investors to understand the fees associated with their investments and to minimize them wherever possible to maximize the power of compounding.

Another important aspect of maximizing the power of compounding is time. The longer the investment horizon, the more time the investor has to benefit from compounding. Even small contributions made consistently over a long period can result in significant growth through compounding. It is essential for investors to start early and stay invested over the long-term to reap the benefits of compounding.

Diversification is another critical factor in maximizing the power of compounding. By diversifying their portfolio across asset classes, geographies, and sectors, investors can reduce their risk and enhance their returns. Diversification can also help investors stay invested during periods of market volatility and ensure they capture the long-term growth potential of various asset classes.

Finally, it's important to understand the impact of inflation on investment returns. Inflation erodes the purchasing power of money over time, so it's important for investors to choose investments that offer a return that exceeds the rate of inflation. By choosing investments that provide a real rate of return, investors can maximize the power of compounding and preserve their purchasing power over the long-term.

Overall, understanding the power of compounding and implementing strategies to maximize its potential can be a significant advantage for investors in achieving their financial goals.

One thing that many people may not realize about maximizing the power of compounding is that it requires patience and discipline. Compounding involves allowing your investment returns to generate further returns over time, which can lead to exponential growth. However, this process can take years or even decades to fully realize its potential. As such, it is important to remain committed to your investment plan and to resist the temptation to make frequent changes or withdrawals.

Another key aspect of maximizing the power of compounding is to focus on long-term investments that have the potential for sustained growth. This may involve diversifying your portfolio across different asset classes, such as stocks, bonds, and real estate, and choosing investments that have a track record of delivering consistent returns over time. It may also involve taking on some level of risk in order to achieve higher potential returns.

In addition, it is important to stay vigilant about fees and expenses associated with your investments, as these can eat away at your returns over time. Choosing low-cost index funds or exchange-traded funds (ETFs) can help reduce fees and increase your overall returns.

Finally, regularly contributing to your investment portfolio, whether through a 401(k), IRA, or other investment account, can help maximize the power of compounding. By consistently investing a portion of your income over time, you can take advantage of the power of dollar-cost averaging, which involves buying more shares of an investment when prices are low and fewer when prices are high. This can help smooth out market fluctuations and potentially increase your long-term returns.

Start as early as possible: The earlier you start investing, the more time your money has to compound. Even small contributions over time can add up to significant amounts of wealth thanks to compounding.

Be consistent: Regular contributions to your investments can lead to significant growth over time. Set up automatic contributions so you don't forget or get sidetracked.

Keep fees low: High fees can eat away at your returns and limit the power of compounding. Look for low-cost investments and brokerages to maximize your gains.

Reinvest dividends: If you're investing in dividend-paying stocks or funds, consider reinvesting those dividends to maximize your compounding power. Over time, these small dividends can add up to significant gains.

Don't let emotions drive your decisions: Market fluctuations and volatility can be unnerving, but it's important to remain focused on your long-term goals. Avoid making rash decisions based on short-term movements and trust in the power of compounding to work in your favor over time.

Take advantage of tax-advantaged accounts: Consider investing in tax-advantaged retirement accounts, such as a 401(k) or IRA. These accounts offer tax benefits that can help your investments grow even faster over time.

Stay diversified: Diversification is important in any investment portfolio, as it helps to reduce risk and maximize returns over the long term. Consider investing in a mix of asset classes, including stocks, bonds, and other investments, to keep your portfolio well-balanced and primed for growth.

By following these tips, you can harness the power of compounding to build wealth over time and achieve your long-term financial goals.

Developing a long-term investment plan

Developing a long-term investment plan is a crucial step in achieving financial goals and securing a stable future. Many people may not realize that the process of developing a comprehensive plan goes beyond just picking stocks and setting aside money for a rainy day. Here are some things that people may not know about developing a long-term investment plan:

Assessing your financial situation: Before developing an investment plan, it's essential to assess your current financial situation. This includes examining your income, expenses, assets, and liabilities. Understanding your financial situation will help you determine how much you can realistically afford to invest.

Identifying your investment goals: Your investment goals should be specific, measurable, achievable, relevant, and time-bound. You should identify what you want to achieve with your investments, such as retirement savings or funding your child's education.

Determining your risk tolerance: Risk tolerance refers to your ability to handle market fluctuations and investment losses. It's crucial to determine your risk tolerance level because it will impact your investment strategy. Investors with high-risk tolerance may choose to invest in stocks, while those with a low-risk tolerance may choose bonds or other fixed-income securities.

Choosing the right investment vehicle: There are many investment vehicles to choose from, including stocks, bonds, mutual funds, ETFs, and alternative investments. The right investment vehicle will depend on your investment goals, risk tolerance, and time horizon.

Diversifying your portfolio: Diversification is an investment strategy that involves spreading your investments across multiple asset classes, sectors, and geographies. This strategy can help to reduce risk and improve returns over the long term.

Regularly monitoring and adjusting your investment plan: Your investment plan should be regularly reviewed to ensure it remains aligned with your investment goals and risk tolerance. Market conditions can change, and adjustments may be necessary to maintain a balanced and diversified portfolio.

Overall, developing a long-term investment plan involves careful consideration of many factors. It's essential to work with a financial professional who can help you identify your investment goals, assess your risk tolerance, and recommend appropriate investment vehicles and strategies. A well-designed investment plan can help you achieve your financial goals and secure a stable future.

Here are a few things to keep in mind when developing a long-term investment plan:

Revisit your plan regularly: Your investment plan should not be a "set it and forget it" type of document. You should review your plan at least once a year and make adjustments as needed. This might include rebalancing your portfolio, adjusting your asset allocation, or reassessing your risk tolerance.

Consider the tax implications: Taxes can significantly impact your investment returns. When developing your plan, consider the tax implications of each investment. For example, stocks held for over a year are taxed at a lower rate than stocks held for less than a year. Additionally, some investments, such as municipal bonds, are tax-exempt.

Keep costs low: Investment fees and expenses can eat into your returns over time. When developing your plan, look for ways to keep costs low, such as investing in low-cost index funds or ETFs.

Stay disciplined: It can be tempting to deviate from your investment plan when the market is volatile or when you hear about the latest hot stock. However, it's important to stay disciplined and stick to your plan. Remember, investing is a long-term game, and trying to time the market or chase returns can do more harm than good.

Have an emergency fund: Before you start investing for the long-term, make sure you have a solid emergency fund in place. This will ensure that you have money set aside to cover unexpected expenses or income interruptions, so you don't have to dip into your investments prematurely.

Be realistic about your goals: When developing your plan, be realistic about your investment goals and what you can realistically achieve. Don't set yourself up for disappointment by expecting to earn high returns in a short amount of time. Instead, focus on creating a plan that aligns with your risk tolerance and long-term financial goals.

How to manage risk in a compounding portfolio

Managing risk is an important aspect of any investment strategy, especially when compounding over the long-term. Here are some key points that many people may not be aware of when it comes to managing risk in a compounding portfolio:

Diversification is key: A diversified portfolio can help spread risk across different assets, sectors, and regions. By investing in a variety of assets that have low correlations to each other, you can reduce the risk of any single asset or market affecting the overall performance of your portfolio.

Understand the risks associated with each investment: Every investment carries risks, and it's important to understand the specific risks associated with each investment in your portfolio. For example, equities can be volatile, bonds can be impacted by changes in interest rates, and cryptocurrencies can be highly speculative. Understanding these risks can help you make more informed investment decisions.

Maintain a long-term focus: Short-term market movements can be unpredictable, but over the long-term, markets have historically trended upward. By maintaining a long-term focus and staying committed to your investment plan, you can avoid the temptation to make impulsive decisions based on short-term market movements.

Consider the impact of fees: Fees and expenses associated with investing can eat into your returns over time. Be sure to understand the fees associated with any investment you make and choose investments with low fees when possible.

Rebalance regularly: As assets in your portfolio grow or decline in value, the allocation of your portfolio can shift over time. Rebalancing your portfolio on a regular basis can help you maintain your desired level of risk exposure and keep your portfolio aligned with your long-term investment goals.

Consider incorporating risk management strategies: There are various risk management strategies that you can consider incorporating into your investment plan, such as stop-loss orders, put options, and other hedging strategies. However, these strategies can be complex and may not be suitable for all investors, so it's important to do your research and consult with a financial professional before implementing them in your portfolio.

Additional points to consider when managing risk in a compounding portfolio:

Diversify your investments: One of the best ways to manage risk is to diversify your investments across different asset classes, sectors, and geographies. This helps to spread your risk across a range of investments and reduces the impact of any single investment on your portfolio.

Use asset allocation: Asset allocation is the process of dividing your portfolio among different asset classes, such as stocks, bonds, and cash. By spreading your investments across different asset classes, you can help manage risk and potentially improve your returns over the long term.

Consider risk tolerance: Your risk tolerance is the level of risk you are comfortable taking on in your investments. It is important to consider your risk tolerance when developing your investment plan, as investing in assets that are too risky can lead to losses that are difficult to recover from.

Stay disciplined: It is important to stick to your investment plan and avoid making impulsive decisions based on short-term market fluctuations. Staying disciplined and focused on your long-term goals can help you manage risk and improve your chances of long-term success.

Monitor your portfolio regularly: It is important to regularly review and monitor your portfolio to ensure it remains aligned with your investment plan and risk tolerance. Rebalancing your portfolio from time to time can help you maintain your desired asset allocation and manage risk over the long term.

Seek professional advice: If you are uncertain about managing risk in your portfolio, seeking advice from a professional financial advisor can be helpful. They can provide guidance on managing risk and developing an investment plan that is aligned with your goals and risk tolerance.

CHAPTER *13*
THE IMPORTANCE OF PATIENCE AND DISCIPLINE IN LONG-TERM INVESTING

Patience and discipline are two important traits that any long-term investor needs to possess in order to succeed in compounding their investments. Many people tend to overlook or underestimate the importance of these traits, which can lead to poor investment decisions and missed opportunities.

One of the key things that many people do not know about the importance of patience and discipline in long-term investing is that it can be difficult to maintain these traits over long periods of time. It is easy to get caught up in short-term market fluctuations and be tempted to make impulsive investment decisions based on emotions rather than sound financial analysis.

However, successful long-term investors understand that investing is a marathon, not a sprint. They take a long-term perspective and are patient in their approach to investing. They recognize that short-term fluctuations in the market are normal and do not allow these fluctuations to sway their investment decisions.

Furthermore, long-term investors also understand the importance of discipline in sticking to their investment plan. They have a clear investment strategy and stick to it, regardless of short-term market movements or popular investment fads. This allows them to remain focused on their long-term investment goals and avoid making impulsive investment decisions that could negatively impact their investment returns.

In addition, successful long-term investors also understand the power of compounding and the importance of giving their investments time to grow. They are patient and disciplined enough to allow their investments to compound over long periods of time, which can result in significant wealth accumulation.

Overall, the importance of patience and discipline in long-term investing cannot be overstated. These traits allow investors to maintain a long-term perspective, avoid making impulsive investment decisions, and give their investments time to compound and grow over time.

Here are additional points on the importance of patience and discipline in long-term investing:

Avoid emotional reactions: Patience and discipline help investors avoid emotional reactions to market events. When prices drop, many investors panic and sell, often at a loss. By maintaining a long-term perspective, investors can resist the temptation to make short-term decisions based on emotions.

Avoiding emotional reactions is an important aspect of successful long-term investing, yet many people struggle with this. One thing that many people may not know is that humans are wired to respond emotionally to financial information, and this can lead to poor investment decisions.

For example, when the market is going up, it can be easy to get caught up in the excitement and buy stocks that are overvalued. Similarly, when the market is going down, it can be easy to panic and sell stocks that are undervalued. These emotional reactions can lead to buying high and selling low, which is the opposite of what a successful long-term investor should do.

To avoid emotional reactions, it is important to have a solid investment plan in place and to stick to that plan regardless of short-term market fluctuations. This means avoiding impulsive buying and selling based on fear or excitement, and instead making decisions based on data and analysis.

Another way to avoid emotional reactions is to have a long-term perspective. By focusing on the long-term potential of an investment, investors can avoid getting caught up in short-term market fluctuations and remain committed to their investment plan.

Finally, it is important to recognize that there will be ups and downs in the market, and to avoid making investment decisions based on fear or greed. Instead, successful long-term investors are patient and disciplined, and they avoid making rash decisions based on emotional reactions.

Be aware of your biases: Many investors are susceptible to cognitive biases, which can lead to irrational decisions. Some common biases include confirmation bias (only seeking information that confirms pre-existing beliefs), overconfidence bias (thinking you know more than you actually do), and loss aversion bias (feeling the pain of losses more than the pleasure of gains). By being aware of your biases, you can work to mitigate their effects on your decision-making.

Stick to your plan: Having a long-term investment plan can help you stay on track and avoid making impulsive decisions based on short-term market fluctuations. It's important to have a plan that aligns with your investment goals and risk tolerance, and to stick to that plan even during times of market volatility.

Avoid reacting to news headlines: Financial news outlets often sensationalize market events, and it can be easy to react emotionally to news headlines. Instead of making investment decisions based on news reports, take a step back and look at the bigger picture. Consider how the news may impact the long-term prospects of the companies or markets you are invested in.

Use technology to your advantage

Technology can help you avoid making emotional decisions by automating your investment strategy. For example, you can set up automatic contributions to your investment accounts, which can help you avoid the temptation to stop investing during market downturns.

Using technology to your advantage is a powerful tool when it comes to long-term investing. Many people don't realize the numerous ways in which technology can assist with investing, and the benefits it can provide for a compounding portfolio. Here are some things that many people might not know about this topic:

Access to more information: Technology has made it easier than ever to access information about different stocks, bonds, and other investment opportunities. There are numerous online resources and tools available, such as stock market analysis tools, financial news websites, and online communities of investors, which can help you stay up-to-date on the latest news and trends in the investing world.

Automated investing: Many investment platforms offer automated investing options that use algorithms and machine learning to select and manage a diversified portfolio of investments. This can help you take the emotion out of investing and ensure that your investments are managed efficiently.

Portfolio management tools: There are a variety of online tools and software programs that can help you manage your investment portfolio, track your performance, and make informed decisions about rebalancing your holdings. These tools can save time and provide valuable insights into your investment strategy.

Mobile apps: Mobile apps allow you to access your investment accounts on-the-go, monitor your portfolio performance, and receive real-time updates on the market. Some apps even offer features such as automated alerts for price changes or market news, making it easier to stay informed and make informed investment decisions.

Robo-advisors: Robo-advisors are online investment management services that use algorithms to create and manage investment portfolios for clients. These services typically offer lower fees than traditional financial advisors, making them an affordable option for many investors.

By taking advantage of technology, investors can gain access to more information, make informed decisions, and manage their portfolios more efficiently. It is important to keep in mind, however, that technology is not a substitute for sound investment strategies and disciplined decision-making.

Some additional things people may not know about using technology to their advantage in investing:

Robo-advisors: Robo-advisors are computer programs that use algorithms to help investors select and manage their portfolios. They typically charge lower fees than human financial advisors and can be a good option for those just starting out with investing or for those who want a more hands-off approach to managing their investments.

Online tools and resources: There are many online tools and resources available to investors, including stock and bond screeners, financial calculators, and investment news and analysis. These can help investors make more informed investment decisions and stay up-to-date on market trends.

Mobile apps: Many brokerages and investment firms offer mobile apps that allow investors to manage their portfolios from their smartphones or tablets. These apps can provide real-time market data, news and alerts, and the ability to buy and sell securities on the go.

Social media: Social media platforms like Twitter and LinkedIn can be valuable resources for investors, allowing them to connect with other investors and industry experts, share information and ideas, and stay up-to-date on market news and trends.

Artificial intelligence: Artificial intelligence (AI) is increasingly being used in investing to analyze market data, identify patterns, and make predictions about future market trends. While AI can be a powerful tool for investors, it is important to use it in conjunction with other sources of information and analysis to make informed investment decisions.

Practice mindfulness: Mindfulness can help you stay present and aware of your thoughts and emotions. By practicing mindfulness, you can develop a greater awareness of how your emotions are impacting your investment decisions, and learn to respond to market events in a more measured and rational way.

Recognize the power of compounding: The longer an investment is held, the greater the potential for compounding returns. Investors who remain patient and stay invested for the long term can benefit from the power of compounding, which can help their investments grow exponentially over time.

Don't try to time the market

Trying to time the market by buying and selling based on short-term fluctuations is a losing strategy. Investors who try to time the market often end up buying high and selling low, missing out on potential gains over the long term. Instead, investors should focus on their long-term goals and avoid trying to predict short-term market movements.

"Don't try to time the market" is a well-known piece of investment advice that recommends investors not to attempt to buy and sell assets based on predictions about future price movements. Instead, the advice suggests that investors should maintain a consistent approach to their investments over the long-term, regardless of short-term fluctuations in the market.

Many people do not know that attempting to time the market can be a challenging and risky strategy. Even professional investors who have access to extensive resources and data have difficulty predicting market trends accurately. Studies have shown that timing the market requires investors to be correct twice, first in knowing when to sell and then when to buy back. In practice, it is often challenging to get both calls right.

Additionally, trying to time the market can lead to missed opportunities for growth, as investors who wait on the sidelines may miss out on market gains. On the other hand, those who attempt to time the market may also expose themselves to losses if they sell at the wrong time, and markets do not recover as expected.

Another aspect many people may not be aware of is that attempting to time the market can also be emotionally taxing. It can lead to decision fatigue, stress, and anxiety, especially if an investor constantly checks the markets and feels compelled to make decisions based on every move. Emotion-driven decisions can lead to costly mistakes and detract from long-term goals.

Instead of trying to time the market, a better approach is to maintain a well-diversified portfolio, follow a disciplined investment plan, and focus on long-term goals. This way, investors can take advantage of the power of compounding and avoid the risks and uncertainties that come with market timing.

Trying to time the market is the practice of buying or selling securities based on predicting the market's future movements. This is a very difficult practice, as it requires predicting the behavior of millions of investors, the actions of companies and governments, and the impact of global events, all of which can be very difficult to predict.

Many people do not realize that market timing is a losing game. Studies have shown that attempts to time the market typically lead to lower returns than a buy-and-hold strategy, even when the timing is done by professionals. In fact, research has shown that most market gains come from a small number of days, and missing out on those days can significantly reduce returns over the long term.

Furthermore, market timing can lead to emotional reactions and irrational decision-making, which can cause investors to buy high and sell low. This can lead to significant losses and missed opportunities for gains.

Instead of trying to time the market, investors should focus on building a diversified portfolio of high-quality investments, with a focus on long-term growth and compounding. This strategy can help investors ride out short-term market fluctuations and capture the long-term returns of the market.

Diversify: Diversification is a key component of a long-term investment plan. By spreading their investments across different asset classes and sectors, investors can help manage risk and reduce the impact of any single investment on their portfolio. This can help investors stay disciplined during market fluctuations and avoid making emotional decisions based on short-term market movements.

CHAPTER *14*

THE IMPORTANCE OF PATIENCE AND DISCIPLINE IN LONG-TERM INVESTING

The importance of patience and discipline in long-term investing cannot be overstated. Many investors fall prey to the temptation to buy and sell assets based on short-term market fluctuations or news events, rather than sticking to a well-thought-out long-term investment plan.

One of the keys to successful long-term investing is to maintain a patient and disciplined approach, particularly during times of market volatility or uncertainty. This means being willing to ride out short-term fluctuations in the market, rather than making knee-jerk reactions based on fear or anxiety.

Another important aspect of patience and discipline in long-term investing is the ability to stay focused on your long-term goals and not get distracted by short-term market noise. This requires a solid understanding of your own investment goals, risk tolerance, and investment time horizon, as well as a well-constructed investment plan that takes these factors into account.

Additionally, it's important to remember that successful long-term investing is not a one-time event but rather a continuous process that requires ongoing attention and adjustment. This means regularly reviewing and rebalancing your portfolio to ensure that it remains aligned with your long-term goals, risk tolerance, and investment time horizon.

Patience and discipline in long-term investing requires a certain level of emotional detachment from your investments. This means not getting too attached to any one asset or investment and being willing to make changes to your portfolio as needed, even if it means selling assets that you may be emotionally attached to. By maintaining a level-headed, disciplined approach to investing, you'll be better equipped to make sound, rational investment decisions that can help you achieve your long-term financial goals.

Stay focused on the long-term: One of the most critical factors for successful long-term investing is to have a clear understanding of your goals and investment time horizon. This enables you to make investment decisions based on a long-term perspective rather than reacting to short-term market movements.

Stick to your investment plan

Once you have established your long-term investment plan, it is crucial to stick to it. Avoid making impulsive or emotional investment decisions based on short-term market movements or news. Stay disciplined and focused on your investment objectives.

When it comes to investing, it's important to have a plan and stick to it. This means setting clear goals, choosing the right investment vehicles, and determining a time horizon for your investments. However, many people may not fully understand the importance of sticking to their investment plan.

One thing many people may not realize is that sticking to an investment plan can help to reduce emotional reactions to market volatility. When markets are fluctuating, it can be tempting to make knee-jerk reactions and sell off assets in a panic. However, this can often be a mistake, as it may lead to missed opportunities for long-term growth. By having a clear investment plan in place, you can avoid making decisions based on emotions and instead make rational choices based on your goals and objectives.

Another benefit of sticking to an investment plan is that it can help to reduce the impact of behavioral biases. Behavioral biases are common psychological tendencies that can cause investors to make irrational decisions. For example, the fear of missing out (FOMO) can cause investors to chase after hot stocks or other assets that are rising in value, even if they don't align with their long-term investment goals. On the other hand, the fear of loss (FOL) can cause investors to panic and sell off assets during market downturns, even if they were initially part of a long-term investment plan. By sticking to your investment plan, you can avoid falling prey to these and other behavioral biases.

Sticking to an investment plan can help to ensure that you are staying on track toward your long-term goals. It can be easy to get sidetracked by short-term fluctuations and news headlines, but by sticking to your plan, you can stay focused on your larger objectives. This can help to ensure that you are making progress toward your goals over time, even if there are bumps in the road along the way.

Overall, sticking to your investment plan is crucial for achieving long-term success in investing. It can help to reduce emotional reactions to market volatility, reduce the impact of behavioral biases, and keep you on track toward your larger objectives.

Embrace volatility

The stock market is inherently volatile, and it can be unsettling to see your portfolio value fluctuate. However, it is essential to remember that volatility is a normal part of long-term investing. The key is to stay invested and avoid the temptation to make knee-jerk reactions during market downturns.

Embracing volatility is an important principle in long-term investing, but it is often misunderstood or overlooked by many investors. Volatility is a natural and inevitable part of the market, and it can be driven by a range of factors, including economic indicators, global events, and investor sentiment. Rather than being afraid of volatility, long-term investors should embrace it as an opportunity to build wealth over time.

One reason to embrace volatility is that it can create buying opportunities. When the market experiences a downturn, many investors panic and sell their holdings, which can drive prices down even further. However, for long-term investors, this can create an opportunity to purchase high-quality assets at a discounted price. By buying low and holding for the long term, investors can potentially benefit from the eventual recovery of the market and see substantial growth in their portfolio.

Another reason to embrace volatility is that it can help investors avoid the temptation to time the market. Trying to predict market trends and buy or sell based on those predictions can be a dangerous game, as even the most experienced investors cannot accurately predict market movements. By embracing volatility and sticking to a long-term investment plan, investors can avoid the urge to try to time the market and instead focus on building a well-diversified portfolio that can weather short-term market fluctuations.

Ultimately, embracing volatility is about recognizing that short-term market fluctuations are a normal part of investing and that a long-term investment strategy can help to minimize the impact of market volatility on your portfolio. By staying disciplined, maintaining a diversified portfolio, and focusing on your long-term goals, you can build wealth over time and benefit from the power of compounding.

Embracing volatility can be challenging for many investors who may have been taught to view market fluctuations as a negative thing. However, it is important to remember that volatility is a normal and necessary part of the investment process. In fact, volatility can create opportunities for investors to buy assets at discounted prices or to sell assets at a premium.

One of the key benefits of embracing volatility is that it can help investors to achieve their long-term financial goals. This is because the compounding effect of reinvesting gains can be much more powerful when investors are able to buy assets at lower prices. By staying disciplined and investing consistently over the long term, investors can benefit from the power of compounding and achieve significant gains over time.

Another benefit of embracing volatility is that it can help investors to build emotional resilience. By becoming more comfortable with market fluctuations, investors can avoid making impulsive decisions based on short-term market movements. This can help them to stay on track with their long-term investment plan and avoid costly mistakes.

One strategy for embracing volatility is to maintain a well-diversified investment portfolio. By spreading investments across a range of asset classes, geographies, and sectors, investors can reduce their exposure to any one particular market or asset. This can help to mitigate risk and reduce the impact of market fluctuations on the overall portfolio.

Ultimately, embracing volatility is about recognizing that short-term market movements are not always an accurate reflection of an asset's long-term potential. By maintaining a disciplined and patient approach to investing, investors can benefit from the long-term compounding effects of their investments, while minimizing the negative impact of short-term market fluctuations.

Diversify your portfolio

Diversification is an essential component of a long-term investment strategy. By spreading your investments across a variety of asset classes, you can reduce your overall risk and help mitigate the impact of any individual investment that may underperform.

Diversification is a key concept in investing, and it refers to the practice of spreading your investments across different asset classes, sectors, and geographies. The idea behind diversification is to reduce your exposure to any one particular investment, so that if one investment performs poorly, the impact on your overall portfolio is minimized. Many people understand the basic concept of diversification, but there are several important aspects to consider when implementing a diversification strategy:

Asset allocation: One of the most important decisions when diversifying is to determine the appropriate mix of asset classes for your portfolio. Common asset classes include stocks, bonds, real estate, and commodities. Each asset class has its own characteristics in terms of risk and return, and finding the right balance for your goals and risk tolerance is crucial.

Geographic diversification: Investing in different countries can reduce risk by minimizing exposure to any one particular market. It is important to consider both developed and emerging markets in order to achieve true geographic diversification.

Sector diversification: Within each asset class, it is important to diversify across different sectors. For example, in the stock market, there are different sectors such as technology, healthcare, and financials. Investing in a mix of sectors can help to reduce your exposure to any one particular sector.

Rebalancing: Over time, your portfolio may become unbalanced as some investments perform better than others. Rebalancing your portfolio involves selling some of your winners and buying more of your losers to get back to your desired asset allocation. This can be a challenging decision to make, but it is important to stick to your long-term investment plan.

Monitoring: Diversification is not a one-time event, but rather an ongoing process. It is important to regularly review and monitor your portfolio to ensure it continues to align with your investment goals and risk tolerance. Regular check-ins can help identify any areas that may need adjustment to keep your portfolio diversified.

Overall, diversification can be a powerful tool for reducing risk in your investment portfolio, and there are many different ways to achieve diversification depending on your goals and risk tolerance. It is important to work with a financial advisor to develop a customized diversification strategy that meets your needs.

Another aspect to diversification that people may not be aware of is the importance of diversifying across different asset classes, not just within the same class. For example, it's not enough to just own a bunch of different stocks - those stocks may all be in the same industry or have similar risk profiles, meaning that if that industry or market segment experiences a downturn, your entire portfolio could suffer.

Instead, it's important to diversify across asset classes, such as stocks, bonds, real estate, and alternative investments like commodities or cryptocurrency. Each of these classes has different risk and return profiles, so having exposure to a variety of them can help spread out your risk and reduce the impact of any one class experiencing a downturn.

Additionally, it's important to remember that diversification is not a one-and-done activity - it's something that needs to be monitored and adjusted over time as market conditions and your own financial situation changes. Rebalancing your portfolio regularly can help ensure that you are still properly diversified and taking advantage of new opportunities for growth.

Be patient and don't get greedy

Patience is key to successful long-term investing. It can be tempting to try to time the market or chase high returns, but these strategies often lead to losses. Be patient, stick to your investment plan, and avoid getting greedy by trying to achieve unrealistic returns in a short period.

When it comes to investing, many people make the mistake of letting greed take over and attempting to make large profits in a short amount of time. However, this often leads to making impulsive decisions, taking unnecessary risks, and ultimately losing money.

Being patient and avoiding greed is crucial when it comes to long-term investing. It's important to understand that investing is a slow and steady process, and it's not a get-rich-quick scheme. Instead, investing should be viewed as a way to gradually build wealth over time.

To avoid getting greedy, it's important to set realistic expectations for your investments and stick to your long-term investment plan. Don't let short-term gains or losses distract you from your overall investment goals. Additionally, it's important to avoid chasing after the latest hot stock or market trend, as this often leads to making emotional investment decisions and taking on unnecessary risks.

Another way to avoid getting greedy is to maintain a diversified portfolio. By spreading your investments across a variety of asset classes, you can minimize your overall risk and avoid putting all your eggs in one basket. This can help you avoid getting too attached to any one particular investment, and it can also help you avoid chasing after high-risk, high-reward opportunities.

Being patient, setting realistic expectations, sticking to your investment plan, and maintaining a diversified portfolio are all important ways to avoid getting greedy and to ensure long-term investment success.

Regularly review your portfolio: While it is essential to remain disciplined and patient, it is also important to regularly review your portfolio and adjust your investment strategy as needed. This may involve rebalancing your portfolio or making changes based on changes in your investment objectives or life circumstances.

The key to successful long-term investing is to remain disciplined, patient, and focused on your investment objectives. By embracing volatility, diversifying your portfolio, and avoiding impulsive decisions, you can increase your chances of achieving your long-term financial goals.

The potential pitfalls of short-term thinking and trading

Short-term thinking and trading can be alluring to investors, as it can provide the potential for quick profits. However, there are many potential pitfalls to this approach that many people may not be aware of.

One of the main risks of short-term thinking and trading is that it can be difficult to consistently predict short-term price movements. This can lead to losses if investors make trades based on short-term trends that ultimately turn against them. Additionally, frequent trading can also lead to high transaction costs, such as trading fees and taxes, which can eat into profits.

Another risk is that short-term trading can cause investors to miss out on the long-term growth potential of certain investments. This is because short-term market volatility can cause significant price fluctuations, but over the long-term, the overall trend may be upwards. By focusing solely on short-term price movements, investors may miss out on the long-term growth potential of certain investments.

Furthermore, short-term thinking and trading can also lead to emotional decision-making, which can be detrimental to a portfolio's performance. Emotions such as fear and greed can cause investors to make irrational decisions, such as selling low and buying high. This can lead to significant losses and underperformance compared to a more disciplined, long-term approach.

Overall, it is important to carefully consider the potential risks and benefits of short-term thinking and trading before engaging in these activities. In many cases, a long-term investment strategy that focuses on fundamental analysis and a diversified portfolio can be more effective in achieving sustainable growth and mitigating risk.

Certainly! One potential pitfall of short-term thinking and trading is that it can lead to emotional decision-making. When investors are focused on short-term gains or losses, they may be more likely to make impulsive decisions based on fear, greed, or other emotions, rather than sticking to a disciplined, long-term investment strategy.

Another potential pitfall is that short-term trading can be more costly due to transaction fees, which can eat into potential profits. Additionally, short-term trading requires more frequent monitoring and research, which can be time-consuming and stressful.

Short-term trading can also be riskier, as prices can be more volatile in the short term. Trying to time the market or predict short-term price movements is notoriously difficult and can result in significant losses if the investor makes the wrong call.

Finally, short-term trading can distract investors from their long-term goals, leading to a lack of focus and discipline in their overall investment strategy. By constantly chasing short-term gains, investors may miss out on the bigger picture and the potential for long-term, sustainable growth.

PART 7
THE POWER OF COMPOUNDING IN ACHIEVING LONG-TERM WEALTH GROWTH

CHAPTER *15*

THE POWER OF COMPOUNDING IN ACHIEVING LONG-TERM WEALTH GROWTH

The power of compounding is a concept that can lead to significant wealth growth over time. Many people understand the basic idea of compounding: reinvesting earnings on an investment to earn more earnings in the future. However, there are some key aspects of compounding that many people may not fully understand.

Firstly, one of the most important factors in compounding is time. The longer an investment is left to compound, the greater the potential for growth. This is why starting to invest early in life is so important, as it allows for more time to take advantage of compounding.

Another important aspect of compounding is the rate of return. Even small differences in the rate of return can make a big difference in the long run. For example, an investment that earns an average annual return of 7% will double in value in approximately 10 years, while an investment that earns an average annual return of 10% will double in value in just over 7 years.

It's also important to note that compounding doesn't just apply to investments. It can also apply to debt. When interest is compounded on debt, it can quickly grow into a much larger amount, making it much harder to pay off over time. This is why it's important to pay off debt as soon as possible to avoid compounding interest from becoming a burden.

In addition, it's worth noting that while compounding can lead to significant wealth growth over time, it's not a guarantee. Investments can go up and down in value, and there is always a risk involved. It's important to do your research, diversify your investments, and have a long-term strategy to make the most of the power of compounding.

Time is key: The longer you can let your investments compound, the more time they have to grow. This means that starting early is crucial, as even small amounts can grow into significant wealth over long periods of time.

Regular investments: Making regular, consistent contributions to your investments allows for even greater compounding, as you are continually adding to your principal balance. This is known as dollar-cost averaging and can help to smooth out fluctuations in the market.

Reinvest dividends: Reinvesting dividends allows you to take advantage of compounding even further. By automatically reinvesting dividends back into the investment, you are able to purchase additional shares, which can grow in value over time.

Consider tax implications: It's important to understand the tax implications of compounding investments. Certain types of accounts, such as individual retirement accounts (IRAs) and 401(k)s, offer tax advantages that can help your investments grow even more.

Risk vs. reward

Compounding can be powerful, but it's important to understand that higher returns often come with higher risks. Understanding your risk tolerance and creating a diversified portfolio can help you manage risk while still taking advantage of the power of compounding.

Risk and reward are two important factors that every investor should consider when making investment decisions. Risk refers to the possibility that an investment will lose value or fail to achieve the expected return, while reward is the potential gain an investor may receive from that investment.

One thing that many people may not know about risk vs. reward is that the two factors are often closely related. In general, the greater the potential reward, the greater the risk involved. This is because higher-risk investments, such as stocks or cryptocurrencies, often have the potential for higher returns than lower-risk investments, such as bonds or savings accounts.

It's also important to note that risk and reward are not the only factors to consider when making investment decisions. Other important factors may include an investor's financial goals, time horizon, and risk tolerance. For example, an investor with a longer time horizon may be willing to take on more risk in exchange for the potential for higher returns, while an investor with a shorter time horizon may be more focused on preserving capital and generating income.

Ultimately, every investment carries some degree of risk, and it's up to each individual investor to decide how much risk they are comfortable taking on in pursuit of their investment goals. By carefully weighing the potential risks and rewards of different investment options, investors can make informed decisions and build a portfolio that aligns with their long-term financial goals.

When it comes to risk vs. reward, it's important to keep in mind that they are inherently linked in the world of investing. Higher returns typically come with a higher level of risk, and lower risk investments typically come with lower returns. However, many people do not fully understand the relationship between risk and reward and the implications it can have for their investment strategies.

One common mistake is assuming that higher risk always leads to higher rewards. This is not necessarily true, as there is always the possibility of losing money when investing, regardless of the risk level. Additionally, there are often hidden costs associated with high-risk investments, such as higher fees or lower liquidity.

On the other hand, some investors may be too risk-averse and only invest in low-risk options, such as bonds or savings accounts. While these investments may be less volatile, they may not offer the same potential for growth as higher-risk investments.

Ultimately, the key is to find a balance between risk and reward that aligns with your personal goals, financial situation, and risk tolerance. It's important to have a diversified portfolio that includes a mix of high and low-risk investments, and to regularly reassess your portfolio to ensure it is still aligned with your goals and risk tolerance. It's also important to remember that risk and reward are not the only factors to consider when investing, and other factors such as liquidity, fees, and tax implications should also be taken into account.

Consistency is key: Sticking to your long-term investment plan and resisting the temptation to make frequent changes in response to short-term market fluctuations is crucial to the success of compounding. By consistently contributing to your investments and staying invested through market cycles, you can achieve long-term wealth growth.

Why starting early and staying the course is key

Starting early and staying the course are key components of successful long-term investing, but many people do not fully understand the reasons why.

One reason why starting early is important is that it allows for more time for compounding to work its magic. The earlier you start, the more time your investments have to grow and compound over time, which can result in significant wealth accumulation in the long run. On the other hand, if you delay investing, you miss out on this crucial time and can potentially miss out on significant returns.

Another reason why staying the course is important is because it helps you avoid making emotional decisions based on short-term market fluctuations. When you stay invested for the long term, you are less likely to react to short-term market volatility and make rash decisions that can harm your portfolio. Additionally, staying invested for the long term allows you to ride out market downturns and recover from losses, which is important for achieving long-term growth.

Finally, starting early and staying the course can help you establish good investing habits and discipline. By starting early and committing to a long-term investment plan, you can develop the patience and discipline needed to successfully navigate the ups and downs of the market and achieve your financial goals over time. This can be especially valuable in today's fast-paced world, where people are often tempted to seek quick gains or react impulsively to market changes.

One thing that many people may not realize is just how much of an impact starting early can have on the long-term growth of their investments. By starting to invest at a younger age, even if only with small amounts, you have more time for the power of compounding to work its magic.

For example, let's say you start investing $1,000 per year at the age of 25, and you continue to do so until you reach the age of 65. Assuming an average annual return of 7%, your initial investment of $40,000 would have grown to over $350,000 by the time you reach 65. However, if you wait until you're 35 to start investing that same $1,000 per year, you would only have around $165,000 by the time you're 65, even with the same average annual return.

This is because the earlier you start investing, the longer your investments have to grow and compound. Even small amounts can make a big difference over time. And by staying the course and continuing to invest regularly over the long term, you can benefit from the full potential of compounding to help you achieve your financial goals.

Final thoughts and recommendations

"The Power of Compounding: Achieving Exponential Wealth Growth through Investment Strategies" provides a comprehensive and insightful guide to understanding the power of compounding and developing a successful long-term investment plan. The book covers a wide range of topics, from the basics of investing and compounding to more advanced strategies for managing risk and maximizing returns.

One of the book's key strengths is its focus on the importance of patience and discipline in long-term investing. It emphasizes the need to develop a clear investment plan and stick to it, rather than succumbing to emotional reactions or trying to time the market. The book also stresses the importance of diversification and embracing volatility as a means of maximizing the power of compounding.

Overall, "The Power of Compounding" is an excellent resource for anyone looking to build long-term wealth through investing. It offers practical advice and strategies that can be applied by investors of all levels, from beginners to seasoned professionals. I highly recommend this book to anyone who wants to achieve exponential wealth growth and take control of their financial future.

www.ingramcontent.com/pod-product-compliance
Lightning Source LLC
Chambersburg PA
CBHW020437220526
45464CB00002B/744